Goodbye Kit

*It may be for years
and it may be forever*

Michael C Kickham
1861 – 1909 : A Memoir

Vincent Murphy

Flag Lane Publishers

Published by:
Flag Lane Publishers
3 Elm Bank, Cork
Ireland
www.flaglane.ie

To comment on the book or to leave a review, please visit the above website comments page. All comments and reviews welcome.

ISBN: 978-1-7398589-0-2

Reader Reviews

Goodbye Kit, Vincent Murphy's imagined retelling of his grand uncle's story is the product of meticulous research and a dedicated quest to unearth details of his ancestor Michael Kickham, whose life journey took him from Co. Tipperary to Buneos Aires via New Zealand and Australia in the latter part of the 19th century.

The joy of this book is the extraordinary treasure trove of letters and contemporaneous newspaper articles through which the voice of a young man, dead for over a century, shines through. Described in his lifetime as 'eloquent and impressive' Michael Kickham's letters have an immediacy that bring history to life. Fenians, the Land League and Parnell are topics of the day even far away in New Zealand.

The very worldly challenges of income and prospects within the church are highlighted. The gradual disillusionment of 'the good priest and staunch patriot', disputes with Bishops, petitions to the Vatican, are all charted. From the beginning in Mullinahone right to the end in South America Vincent Murphy has relentlessly pursued his quest to piece together the story of the man behind the letters. A most interesting read.

'I was of course all alone, mountains before, mountains behind, sometimes near the sea so that I could hear it beating on the rocks beneath' [from a letter from Michael to his parents]

Una Leader

I found the book an enjoyable and interesting read. From Fr. Michael's letters it was easy to imagine what life was like living in remote areas in New Zealand and Australia.

His letters give a vivid account of the difficulties he encountered emotionally and physically in carrying out his pastoral duties. The blatant discrimination against secular priests and the unwillingness of the hierarchy to address or acknowledge their concerns gave rise to discontent and anger.

The obvious political and patriotic views of Fr. Michael and other Irish priests for an independent Ireland leapt off the pages.

Although Michael was well thought of and respected within and outside his pastoral care, his own discontent and personal struggles brew beneath the surface.

An enjoyable read, a mystery story that kept me rooting for Michael and engaged to the final page.

Deirdre Fitzgibbon

In *'Goodbye Kit, it may be for years and it may be forever'* the difficulties facing a priest who wanted to leave the priesthood are well illustrated as is the shame that would attach to them and their families. Michael Kickham's internal torment as he considers leaving the priesthood is graphically portrayed. He is all too aware of the consequences.

In 1884, Michael was ordained and sent to New Zealand as a missionary priest, where he discovered an unhappy environment: the diocese was run by Marists who looked down on Secular priests and treated them as 'only there to assist the Marists'. This attitude led to Michael and other Secular priests sending a petition to Pope Leo XIII.

Did the powers that be in All Hallows know this when they sent out young priests as missionaries? And if they did, did they conveniently ignore it? Unfortunately, despite meticulous research by the author, this question remains unanswered.

He returned to Ireland in 1899 and two years later departed for a destination undisclosed to his family. He was eventually found to be in Buenos Aires, no longer a priest. He died there in 1909, just 48 years old.

An interesting and enigmatic life, well told by author Vincent Murphy and a joy to read.

Anne Casey

A fascinating account of an unusual life, this book tells the true story of Fr. Michael Kickham's journey from early life in Mullinahone to missionary work in Australia and New Zealand, conflict with church authorities, and the mysterious last chapter of his life in South America.

In his meticulously researched work, Vincent Murphy brings to life the exploits of his grand uncle, and leaves us wondering about the ultimate fate of his relative. Highly recommended for those with an interest in the history of everyday lives, the book vividly illustrates the magnitude of what was involved in leaving home and family as well as the ordinary lives of people living in "the colonies" in the latter part of the 19th century and into the 20th.

Cian Murphy

During his lifetime, Father Michael Kickham travelled from Ireland to the opposite ends of the earth. Here was a man who was not afraid to confront his Bishop or write to the Pope when circumstances demanded.

Letters from Michael and others form a central part of the story. There is an honesty and simplicity with a very respectful structure to the letters, an art form that is rapidly diminishing with modern technology. The author, a grand-nephew of Michael, was so fortunate that these letters, which span thirty-three years from 1877, were safeguarded by the Kickham family for future generations.

Perhaps they were kept in the hope that someone might pick up the mantle and record his story for young generations to come, long after Michael had passed away. If so, their vision is realised in Vincent Murphy's book.

The author has woven these personal family letters, archive material from various sources and quotations from poems into a memoir which is a joy to read.

Michael Nolan

This is a really interesting account of the life of an Irish Priest on the other side of the world. The original letters are fascinating, the details in them are like gold dust.

I found the section on New Zealand absolutely fascinating. The author really captured the environment in which Michael lived and the tough life he had to endure as a country priest, really tough on someone who seems to have been a high achiever.

The controversy between Marists and Secular Priests was so well portrayed from Michael's view, that it aroused rage at the injustice.

I really enjoyed the book and finding out about a period and a life that was not previously well known to me.

Margaret Madden

About the author

Vincent Murphy, a native of Clonmel and living in Cork, is a retired Chartered Engineer. He is interested in family research, writing, hill walking, sailing, travel and photography. This current book is the result of extensive research into the life of Michael Kickham, who had a very interesting and enigmatic life. He has also produced:

A Patagonian Odyssey : memories of a hitching trip in 1981, recounting his experience as a lone traveller hitchhiking in winter in 1981.

Me and my relations: a family history

Southwards: a narrative and photographic record of a trip with his wife, Sarah, to Falkland Islands / Islas Malvinas, South Georgia, Antarctic Peninsula and Chile – being re-worked for publication.

Picos de Europa: narrative and photographic record of a hill walking expedition to the Picos de Europa National Park in Spain. Produced for fellow hill-walkers on the expedition.

In 2010, he was co-founder of the Cork based voluntary organisation *The Next Step*, supporting people who experience depression and mental health difficulties. The Next Step is now part of Cork Mental Health Foundation and Vincent is on the board.

Vincent is currently involved in planning the commemoration of Conor OBrien's circumnavigation of the globe between 1923 and 1925, the first to do so under an Irish flag, in a boat designed by himself. He sailed south of the three capes: Cape of Good Hope, Cape Leeuwin (SW Australia) and Cape Horn, the first person ever to do so in a small craft. He always wrote his name without an apostrophe.

Contents

To Aoife and Maeve

Foreword

I can't define a moment when I decided to write a book about Michael Charles Kickham, my grand uncle. It was more the evolution of an idea than any *Eureka* moment. I had some vague knowledge about his life: a missionary in New Zealand; a row with his Bishop; his return to Ireland before going away, without disclosing his destination; he went to Buenos Aires, left the priesthood and become a teacher. He died there.

My cousin Catherine Delahanty gave me copies of his surviving letters home. More letters were obtained from Church archives in New Zealand, Australia and the Vatican.

Much of the book is written as though it were Michael's autobiography. I felt this would allow for a more interesting story than merely reproducing articles and letters. Writing now in the style of an autobiography about a man who died in 1909 will no doubt raise the question as to whether the voice is authentic.

In my defence, all letters in the book are transcripts of actual letters which were either kept in the family or received from archives. There are no fictitious letters or additions to letters in the book. Many of Michael's letters home contain references to people who are now unknown. I decided to leave these in for completeness. I hope the reader does not find this off-putting or confusing.

Events referred to were reported in local newspapers at the time and available from archives. Speeches quoted were developed from newspaper reports which gave very detailed accounts of what each speaker said at meetings. Conversations in general were imagined from the context.

There are many places where the narrative has been based on the general history of the time. These are undoubtedly subject to my prejudices, conscious or not, despite best effort.

There are few surviving records of Michael's life after 1901. The description of his life in Buenos Aires therefore contains assumptions, based on what limited information I have been able to establish. The chapter *Enigma* sets out the background to and reasons for the assumptions made.

Michael's sister was known as Kattie, but Michael also called her Kit. He called his brother Tommy, while everyone else called him Tom. Both versions of these names are used as appropriate.

At the time, Buenos Aires was written as Buenos Ayres and I have used this spelling throughout the narrative, but Buenos Aires here in the Foreword and in the Appendices.

Notes by chapter at the end of the book will, I hope, answer any questions the reader may have. Where I have been inventive, this is recorded in the notes.

Afterword, "*Writing the book: Serendipity and Hard Graft*" is in part acknowledgements but mostly a description of my journey through research in writing this book. Though challenging and at times frustrating and heart-breaking, I enjoyed every minute of it. I hope you, The Reader, will enjoy the result.

Vincent Murphy
November 2021

1 – Firstborn Son

❋❋❋❋❋❋❋

It is Wednesday 23rd of October 1861. We find ourselves in Ireland, in the small town of Mullinahone in Co. Tipperary, near the border with Co. Kilkenny.

John Kickham and Catherine Kickham *neé* Flynn have been married for a year and are expecting their first child. Catherine feels her time is near and sends for the midwife. Five hours later, in the early hours of Thursday morning, she delivers a baby boy.

The midwife calls John to meet his newborn son. He is very nervous, not sure how to hold such a small delicate infant. The midwife, used to expecting this from men, shows him how. He gazes into his son's eyes in amazement and smiles. Then he sits down on the bed beside Catherine, takes her hand, and tells her how delighted he is. They agree to name him Michael Charles. Michael after John's father and Charles after John's illustrious cousin, Charles J. Kickham.

Tired but overjoyed, Catherine holds her baby and wonders what the future holds for him. "Maybe a priest," she thinks. "It would be such an honour to have a priest in the family."

2 - Last Rites

orty-eight years later, on Friday the 3rd of December 1909, Michael Charles Kickham is seriously ill in the British Hospital in Buenos Ayres, capital city of Argentina.

A friend, Louisa Feeney, comes to visit him. When she sees him, she is visibly distraught. "Oh Michael, you poor man, are you in a lot of pain?"

"Hello Louisa, it's good to see you," Michael replies as he struggles to sit up in the bed. "The pain is not so bad now that they are giving me morphine, but it was excruciating before they brought me in here. Never mind me, tell me, how are you and John and the baby?" he continues.

"We're all fine, thank God, Michael." They talk for a while. Louisa sees two Dominican priests approaching.

"Michael," she says, "I called by Lacordaire College on my way and spoke with Father Murphy and Father Owens and asked them to come here. I thought you might like to receive the sacraments." [1]

Michael replies: "No Louisa, thank you for your concern, but I don't feel like talking to them."

Louisa goes over to tell the Dominicans, then returns to Michael's bedside. "Michael, I hope I haven't offended you, but maybe it's time to put the past behind you. It pains me to think you might die without receiving the sacraments. Please Michael."

"Perhaps you're right," he replies. "I've been thinking about my life since they brought me in here. The doctors aren't saying much, but I sense they don't have a lot of hope for me. Maybe you'll consider me a little hypocritical for thinking of God only now when my life seems in danger, but yes, I would like to talk to a priest. I'm sure those Dominicans are very nice men, however I don't really know them. Louisa, would you mind contacting the Passionist Fathers and ask if Father Francis would visit me?"[2]

"Of course, Michael. He is a lovely man, a great priest."

Later that evening Father Francis arrives at Michael's bedside. "Michael, Michael, I hope you don't mind me saying, but you don't look at all well. Are you in much pain?" They talk for a while. Then:

"Father Francis, I am much troubled and I need to find peace. Like yourself, I was once a priest, even a good priest I think. But I rejected everything before I came to Buenos Ayres. I spent a lot of time going over the many matters troubling me: leaving the priesthood seemed to be my only option. However, the peace I sought continued to elude me. Now that death may be at hand, I feel the need to prepare myself to meet God. Will you hear my confession?"

"I'd be honoured, Michael," he replied, taking his stole from his bag and putting it around his neck. He starts: "In the name of the Father, of the Son and of the Holy Spirit. How long Michael, since your last confession?"

Two hours later he makes the sign of the cross as he grants absolution: "Michael Charles Kickham, *Ego te absolvo a peccatis tuis in nomine Patris et Filii et Spiritus Sancti, Amen.*"

Michael feels a weight lift from him as he drifts off to sleep. Father Francis senses the tranquillity in Michael, his head resting on the pillow, eyes closed. He smiles as he walks away, ever a joy to see peace descending on people after they have prepared themselves to meet their Maker.

Louisa returns the following day with her husband, John and their six month old baby. Michael is dozing, but perks up when he hears them and sees the baby.

"She's beautiful," he says. "she's the image of you Louisa. Is she fully recovered from that infection?"

"Yes, she's thriving now."

"And your new house, how is the work going?"

"Slowly I'm afraid," John replies, "It will be next year before we can move in."

Even this short conversation proves too much for Michael and he lies back again, drifting off to sleep.

Michael's condition continues to deteriorate. Friends who come to visit are shocked when they see him. Mostly they sit there for a while, just to be with him. Sometimes a visitor talks about some memory or other, hoping Michael might still be capable of understanding.

On Sunday afternoon, Father Francis returns. Finding Michael unable to talk, he approaches the nurse and discovers what he suspects, that he is unlikely to make it through the night. He prays and asks for God's grace for Michael before administering the sacrament of Extreme Unction.

In the early hours of Monday 6th December 1909, at about 2 am, the nurse is at Michael's bedside and senses that life is ebbing from him. She calls Doctor Pennington.[3]

Michael may be weak and getting weaker in body, but his spirit remains very much alert.

3 - Michael's Story

❀❀❀❀❀❀

For some while now the struggle between body and soul has been intensifying within me. My body's attempts to retain my soul have become ever more feeble and my soul now senses that the moment of breaking free is at hand.

The nurse is beside my bed and I hear her call out: "Come here doctor, I think Michael is slipping away from us."

Doctor Pennington comes over. I try to say something, but no words will come out.

Suddenly I am bathed in a sea of light, infinitely brighter than the sun. Am I now on a journey from life on earth to the next life? Will I meet St. Peter as he calls me to account before I can be admitted to the glorious presence of my Lord God? Or have I already crossed that threshold to the afterlife?

My mind is racing and my whole life is laid out before me: growing up in Mullinahone; education at Mount Melleray, All Hallows, Angers; a curate and parish priest in New Zealand; the Jesuit novitiate in Melbourne; ministry in various parishes in Australia; my return to Ireland; my recent years here in Buenos Ayres. Every last detail. A life of so many ups and downs.

My first thoughts take me back to my early years as a priest in New Zealand, all of twenty five years ago. Now that death is imminent, or indeed may have occurred, I think of those many sermons of mine which so often focused on the hour of death.

> *Better that you remember the Gospel of St. John:*
> *"For whenever our heart condemns us, God is greater than our heart, and he knows everything"*
> *The day will come when life ebbs from your body, when you draw your last breath, when you realise that your time has come, that it is NOW! And the Lord is waiting for you! What will you say in that moment? "I didn't think you would notice Lord"? Well let me remind you here and now that He is noticing and that He will hold you to account!*

These words are now reverberating inside my head, reprimanding me for my failure to heed my own sermons. No matter. I find comfort in my confession to Father Francis and making my peace with God. I feel prepared to meet my Maker.

If my sermons did not hit home with myself, they certainly impressed others. I can see clearly that report of The New Zealand Tablet when I was a newly ordained priest in Napier:

> *The Rev. Father Kickham has a voice the possession of which by some speakers would be the making of them. He, too, as a preacher is both eloquent and impressive. His sermons betray an evident amount of care in their preparations, being appropriate to the occasion, well thought out, the text never departed from, and the sincerity and earnestness pervading them calculated to impress his hearers. Rev. Father Kickham is no advocate for short sermons, as he generally preaches the best part of an hour.[1]*

So long ago.

4 - Mullinahone

I grew up in Mullinahone in County Tipperary, a village of some 700 inhabitants and a world apart from where I now live in this great metropolis of Buenos Ayres.

Twenty years before I was born, Mullinahone was a thriving town of some 3,000. Then the famine struck. Too many died of starvation and many more emigrated to America, Australia, New Zealand, England. Anywhere they might be able to make a new life for themselves. The famine was a raw topic. The horrors people experienced did not fade easily from memories and if it was spoken about at all, it was in hushed, sombre tones.

But Mullinahone was the centre of my Universe. As the poet C J Boland wrote:

> And the man who was never in Mullinahone
> Shouldn't say he had travelled at all. [1]

It's so strange that I can now see things of which I was never before conscious, even my very first day of life. I was just a few hours old when Father and my Godparents, Judith Kickham and

Michael Byrne, took me to the Church to be baptised.[2] Of course it was Judith who carried me, father being so afraid he might harm such a small delicate baby. But I can see now how he looked at me all the way with a broad smile on his face, proud of his first born son. Mother was resting after the ordeal of my arrival and would not return to church for six weeks, when she would receive the blessing of purification, or be 'churched' as it was often called.

The priest poured water on my forehead and baptised me: *"Michael Charles, ego te baptizo in nomine Patris, et Filii, et Spiritus Sancti."* Thus was I initiated into the fold of the One, Holy, Catholic and Apostolic Church.

I was of course at that moment totally unaware of the solemnity of the occasion and the cold water on my forehead was such a shock that I cried out at the top of my voice, something I've seen so often in my life as a priest.

In time my siblings Lory, Tommy, Nick, Kattie and Ellen were born. Ellen died as an infant. She was never much spoken of. It must have been a tough time, very painful for Mother especially. I remember. I was thirteen years old at the time and I remember there was such sadness around the place.

Lory got consumption as a young man. I was in New Zealand and thought about bringing him out there, the climate would have suited better. However, he died before I could arrange it. He was just twenty-three years old. I think of him often.

At home, Father and Mother were strict, ensuring we always behaved ourselves, learned our lessons and minded our manners. You disobeyed Mother at your peril. Father worked hard, always involved in the General Store, constantly trying to make ends meet. For all that, there was a good atmosphere at home.

I spent many hours in the store with Father, doing jobs and running errands. Farmers, tenants, labourers, came in to buy nails, fence posts, buckets, you name it. And women of the town came to buy their groceries. Commercial travellers called to sell stock and collect their dues. Father always seemed to manage.

5 - Being a Kickham

If I had been a Flynn like my mother or a Tobin like my sister-in-law Cisy, or a Murphy like my brother-in-law Raymie, or indeed almost any name other than Kickham, my name would have had no impact on my life. In Mullinahone the Kickham name was unremarkable, I was just one of the many Kickhams around, all of us related in some way.

However, one of those Kickhams happened to be Charles J Kickham, a writer and patriot of note. Because of this, the Kickham name and my relationship to Charles has often pushed me into the limelight and in truth, conferred on me some undeserved status.

Later on in life, when first introduced to someone, my name was an instant focus of attention.

"Are you related to Charles Kickham the writer?"
"Is the Fenian Charles Kickham a relation of yours?"

Charles was born in 1828. He had a severe accident in his youth: at just thirteen years old, he was sitting by the fire one evening when a spark ignited a flask of gunpowder next to him, which exploded in his face. He was knocked senseless, his face was disfigured, and his hearing and sight were seriously impaired for the rest of his life.

For some reason, the family of Charles was beset by misfortune due to firearms.[1] Charles' brother Tom managed to shoot off his own leg while out shooting birds on Slievenamon. He wanted to give the leg a Christian burial, but the parish priest wouldn't have it. Tom, known to us as 'The Dovey', lived with us for a time.

Just a few months before I was born, Charles' and Tom's father, another John Kickham, died as a result of a firearms accident. After his father died, Tom took over his father's drapery business in the town. Tom's sister Maria married James Cleary. Their two girls Annie and Josie, around my own age, would often come to our house to play.[2] As for Charles himself, neither eyesight nor hearing difficulties could stop him from developing his passions.

There was no better writer than Charles at describing life in rural Ireland. His masterpiece, Knocknagow, tells of the life of the poor Irish peasant and the workings of the Irish land system, highlighting what every Irishman knows, that landlords care nothing for their tenants and that their land agents are greedy and unscrupulous. He also wrote many poems, which were often quite romantic.

He was just seventeen when in 1845 he went to Daniel O'Connell's monster meeting in Thurles. He was initially impressed, but when a split later developed between O'Connell and The Young Irelanders, his sympathies and allegiance changed to the latter.

In July 1848 Thomas Francis Meaghar and others came to the area for a mustering of Young Irelanders Clubs on Slievenamon, some four miles from Mullinahone. Charles heard that there were plans for a rebellion, so he set about making pikes, the only possibility of acquiring weapons. Soon afterwards, John Blake Dillon and William Smith O'Brien arrived with rebellion in mind. Charles got their permission to sound the church bell to signal the start of operations. However it wasn't much of a success and it fizzled out after a few days. He had to go into hiding afterwards.

He wrote for a number of papers, including *The Nation, The Celt, The Irishman, The Shamrock*, and the Fenian paper, *The Irish People*.

In 1858 himself and some other Fenians founded the Irish Republican Brotherhood. In 1865 he was arrested for his part in a planned IRB rebellion, and sentenced to 14 years hard labour. He only served three years before being released early on health grounds. Whatever the expectation of the Crown, gaol did not deflect him from his IRB activities.

In gaol he learned 'finger talking'. People could now communicate with him via signs, a great advantage for a man with his hearing difficulties. His two nieces, Annie and Josie, learned this language and they were his interpreters until 1876, when their family brought them to America.

Growing up I was exposed to all the ideas emanating from O'Connell, the Young Irelanders, the Fenians and the IRB, the Land League and the Home Rule movement, and of course Charles himself. As a result, I developed strong political and nationalist views and opinions. But in truth, this was the case for so many growing up in Ireland back then, and even still. The many Irish here in Buenos Ayres have discussion groups and fund-raising societies to support the Home Rule movement and the Irish Parliamentary Party.

But there is another side to us Kickhams. Back in 1649, so the story goes, a farrier sergeant by the name of Kirkham came over to Ireland with Oliver Cromwell's army. After his appalling rampage through Ireland, Cromwell then expropriated huge tracts of land to pay his army. Kirkham was given 250 acres of this confiscated land in the Barony of Slieveardagh. Over the generations, Kirkham changed to Kickham, and some of those Kickhams converted to Catholicism.

The Catholic nationalist within me is horrified and incensed by what Cromwell did, but I think that any stain on the Kickham name has been long since excised, and more recently in no small measure by the writings and political actions of Charles.

6 - A Vocation

September 1873 brought a change to my life, just a month before my twelfth birthday. Father and mother decided I should be educated by the Cistercians at Mount Melleray.[1]

Mount Melleray

The Monks at Melleray had started a school in 1843 which was particularly focused on the classics, Greek and Latin, as well as music. By now it was a seminary, with the express purpose of fostering vocations to the priesthood. So even at this young age, it seems I was destined to become a priest.

Arriving there I was in awe of the many large buildings. Near the entrance were the school and houses of residence. Next came the dairy and other buildings related to the monks' work on the farm. Then the very imposing main monastery building comprising church, refectory, dormitory, guesthouse, chapter-house and library.

Of course it was in Melleray that I was first asked, by fellow students, monks and teachers alike, whether I was related to the great Charles Kickham.

Melleray was quite a change from the close family life in Mullinahone and it took me some time to adopt. Together with all the other boys, I lived in the houses of residence, where we slept in dormitories with long lines of beds either side. We were strangers at first but friendships soon developed. Not all the boys fitted in. Most, including myself were lonely for home and family for a time. A few found the loneliness too much and they did not continue.

Nearly all the food we ate was produced by the monks on the farm – milk and cheese; potatoes and vegetables; mutton, beef and bacon. Not as tasty as home, but we were well fed.

Summer holidays were spent back in Mullinahone. When I wasn't helping Father in the store, I was rambling over Slievenamon hunting for rabbits or fishing for trout in the Anner. Happy days indeed.

I got on well in Melleray. I was a good student and found the classics, Latin and Greek, fascinating. I also discovered I was quite musical and developed a love for the piano.

Father Ignatius was president of the college, a man for whom I came to have a very high regard. His energy seemed unbounded and his deep spirituality affected everyone. After High Mass on Sundays and Holy Days, we would assemble in the Aula Maxima, where he would lecture us on some religious topic. He had a strong influence on our religious formation, and fostered many a vocation.

I began to think a lot about being a priest. I thought about how great it would be to preach the Gospel and serve God, and how fine it would be to lead, guide and serve my parishioners. I went to talk with Father Ignatius.

"So you feel you would like to be a priest, Michael. It is indeed a great joy and a privilege to feel God is calling you to serve him. What makes you think you have a vocation?"

"When I'm at mass, I feel elated at hearing the word of God, and how I would love to be able to spread it. When I pray every morning and every night, I feel at peace. I think about God all the time and I feel he is talking to me."

"That is very sincerely put, Michael, but perhaps it might pass. Becoming a priest requires a lifelong commitment."

"I'm quite certain of my feelings, Father Ignatius," I replied. I felt very confident about my vocation.

"Well then I think you should continue praying to God for guidance. You are an excellent student and have done well here, but you're still very young, barely fifteen years old. Next year, if you still feel that you have a vocation, that will be time enough."

When I told my parents about my vocation, they were delighted. Having a priest in the family was a matter of great prestige in Ireland. Despite my youth, they decided I should commence studies without delay at All Hallows in Dublin which educated many, many priests for missions all over the world.

A brief encounter

After my last year in Melleray, during the summer before going to All Hallows, I met C. Like myself, she loved rambling over the countryside and we often walked together. [2]

On one occasion we were caught out in a heavy shower and we sheltered under a tree. Our hands brushed off one another and I turned towards her. She looked at me and we held hands, then we kissed lightly on the lips. It was my first, and I must say only, such experience and it felt wonderful.

But afterwards I felt guilty. Here I was, about to commence studying for the priesthood and take a vow of chastity. I told C I couldn't be doing this.

I think of her sometimes, and when I do, one of Charles' poems always comes to mind:

"A Welcome (for Clara)"

She's coming, she's coming! my fancy is roaming,
To cull fairest flowers to strew at her feet;
But oh, had I pinions to sweep the dominions
Of poesy, nothing so bright could I meet
As the loveliness beaming, and ceaselessly streaming
From my darling's blue eyes round her smile's sunny play
And that smile will soon cheer us, those eyes will be near us
Mid the flowers and the bowers and the blossoms of May

Occasionally in a quiet moment I wonder how my life would have turned out if I hadn't been ordained. Would I have gone on to marry C? Or would our friendshipship have faded away as some mere youthful infatuation? Would I have married someone else? And settled down and had children? Some evenings when I call to the Feeneys here in Buenos Ayres and see their family life, I think of what might have been.

All Hallows

All Hallows[3] was going to cost a pretty penny. Bishops in dioceses far and near were always looking for priests to service their growing parishes, and they paid All Hallows to educate young men for ordination. Still, these dioceses only paid part of the cost. The parents of those of us being educated paid fees to make up the balance.[3]

Father had to pay £10 a year for me as well as paying for laundry, repair of clothes, medical advice, bed linen, blankets, towels, books, and ecclesiastical dress. Not every family could afford to have their son educated for the priesthood.

So it was that in September 1877, before my sixteenth birthday, and with a large trunk holding all my belongings, Father took me to Fethard to catch the train for Dublin and All Hallows.

It was my first time being so far from home and Dublin was daunting. At Kingsbridge station, I was overwhelmed - so many people, trams, horse-drawn carriages - all quite intimidating for this country boy. The first tram took me to Sackville Street where I gazed in amazement at Nelson's Pillar. Then another to Drumcondra. It was all so new and exciting. After a long walk up the avenue to All Hallows College I was met by an older clerical student, who had volunteered to welcome us new boys, and show us around the austere and awe-inspiring building. This would be our home for five years.

We had to be ready for the admission exam at nine o'clock next morning. I was very nervous. What would happen if I failed? Would I have to go back to Mullinahone with everyone knowing I was a failure? What then would I do?

There were other boys from Mount Melleray and they too were apprehensive. They were mostly a few years older than me and some wondered what a boy so young was doing there. But there were others as young as me.

We slept in dormitories. I found myself talking to boys from all over Ireland. After each exam we would talk among ourselves about how we got on. I was generally quite satisfied with my answers, but hoped I wasn't deceiving myself.

Later each day we had some time for recreation, more time for talking and getting to know one another. There was a piano in the hall. I gravitated towards it and got every encouragement to try it out. I played a few tunes and quite a few boys sang.

The entrance exam continued for three days. There must have been around 80 of us. We were examined in Latin and Greek; Mathematics, Geometry and Algebra. It was a tough three days, but the monks and teachers in Melleray had taught us well. I felt confident enough, but some of the others had their doubts.

When the results were announced, 41 of us were accepted, including myself and five others from Melleray: Patrick Ahern and his older brother Michael; William Kirby; John Fogarty; and Joseph

Whelan. Joseph wasn't very happy there and left after a short time, but the others stayed and were ordained.

Many boys had long faces and tears. They had not been accepted and had to go home. I felt sorry for them, being rejected. Very capable no doubt, they just hadn't attained the standard set.

Seminary Life

For me at sixteen, the big city of Dublin was quite a change from Mullinahone, and full of wonder. There were big houses, luxurious looking shops, trams, very grand carriages, and lots of people.

Life at All Hallows was structured - classes, study, recreation, walks. Not much time to yourself. After a few months, I was called to see the Dean of Studies, as indeed were all the other first year students in turn.

"You know Michael you will be going on the missions after ordination. Many of our priests go to Australia or New Zealand or the U.S. or Canada where there is a growing need for priests to serve the increasing populations, including many Irish emigrants.

"We expect our priests to be devout and principled, to live their lives to the highest moral and religious standards. Only then can they serve those communities well and ensure their parishioners know, respect and live by the laws of God and our Mother Church. Everything here is directed at this.

"You seem to be getting on well here Michael, I hear favourable reports on your progress. Keep up the good work."

We studied Rhetoric, Philosophy, Humanities and Theology. We learned the Liturgies and the administration of the Sacraments. We studied the Gospels and were instructed in how to prepare and deliver Sermons. We were instructed in Piety and Spirituality. All these were necessary for life as a priest, engaging with parishioners, and spreading the Gospel.

Some matters were strictly enforced - obedience, truthfulness, earnestness, piety. The spiritual directors wanted to cultivate a strong conscience among us students. Any suspicion of pretence in devoutness and spiritual matters was quickly noted and resulted in being summoned before the Dean of Studies for a severe reprimand. Not a pleasant experience.

And English! We spent an awful lot of time learning English. We were lectured on our poor command of the English language.

"Each and every one of you thinks you speak English and wonders why we keep going on about it. Yes you speak some sort of English, but your parishioners in America or Australia or New Zealand or anywhere else won't understand a word of what you are saying. We will teach you the Queen's English and by God you will learn to speak English correctly while you are here."

They were relentless in this. At times you would think Theology or Rhetoric were just by the way. But learn to speak English we did.

I might add, with some lack of modesty, that those of us who came from Melleray were exceptionally well prepared in English, while some others arrived very well prepared in the classics, but with a poor command of English.

We played handball and cricket.

On Wednesdays, we would go on a long walk - down the lanes of Drumcondra, or over towards the Phoenix Park, or sometimes further afield. These walks were very pleasant and on occasions we would finish up with a 'gaudeamus' or 'gaudy'. This was where students and directors came together for the evening with conversations, songs and the piano.

We put on plays for students and staff alike. We learned our lines, how to play our part, paint scenery, get props. A lot of preparation. But when we put on the play, there were high spirits all round, and a *gaudy* afterwards.

We had several of these *gaudy* evenings each year, a great way for us students to know the various priests and directors as ordinary people rather than just as our teachers and directors, and no doubt for them to observe us in unguarded moments. They wanted us to develop confidence and to learn how to behave among our parishioners in our missionary parishes and communities. This interaction was fundamental to our development.

There was however one thing for which we were not prepared: the loneliness and isolation that a priest could experience, even among all his parishioners. This was to affect many priests on the missions, and even nearer home.

I wouldn't want to give the impression that All Hallows was all fun and games. Mostly life there was drab enough with just classes and study. Our life was organised for us, every day our routine was set – time for prayers, for classes, for meals, for study and for recreation. A *gaudy* provided a welcome break from routine.

With all the learning and activities, I did find time to write home.

All Hallows College
Drumcondra
Dublin

Dear Father

I received the half-notes for £7 on yesterday.[4] I could not write immediately as we had to go on a long walk after getting our letters. We had a very long walk but it was a nice one, we were walking pretty hard for about four hours. We went through the greatest part of the park. We went as far as the college that Patrick Mullaly was in. I was going to go in there, but I thought he might not be there.

There is a great strike on all the trains leaving Dublin. There does only the mail leave for Kilkenny every day and the most of the other lines are nearly the same way. We are within about half a mile of the bounds of the city.

We could hear nearby the cars[5] and trams. Did Tramore serve Nicholas or did he get any attack of the pain.

I suppose Ann was not married yet, will she before Christmas.

We will get no vacation until the 25th of June, except two or three days idle here at Christmas.

Hoping that you are all well.
    I remain Dear Father,
            Your fond son
                M C Kickham
    P.S. Send on the other half notes as soon as you get this

[Letter undated]

25

Dear Father,

I received your letter on yesterday and was glad to hear you are all well. I got the certificate, I suppose Fr. Hickey wouldn't lose a penny by sending it himself.

We will have a spree on next Saturday, there will be no fast here. We will get a bottle of wine between every three & a big jug of punch to every table of ten. We all have to carve in our turn. I will be carving next week.

If you have not sent the trousers yet send a pair of suspenders with it & a couple of squares of scrap.

I suppose you will not ever get the book Uncle Thomas sent.

I have no time to say any more but I hope you are all well.

Your fond son

Michael Kickham

All Hallows College
Drumcondra Dublin
October 5th 1879

Dear Parents

I received your letter today and the money. I was indeed surprised that Nick was gone to Clonmell. You did not tell me whether you had to pay anything & how much, or did you get a letter from Farrell. Be sure to tell me all when you write next.

You told me nothing about the reason Julie left the convent, but she left it, when you write send me all the news. I will write to Uncle Edmond in a few days & I am going to write to Nick today. I am getting good health.

I did not hear anything about Charles since. Meagher from the river, that was in Thurles is here since the beginning of September. The first evening I saw him I did not know who he was, but I found out afterwards.

I hope you are all well. The cap will do splendidly, you need not mind the tassel.

Your affectionate son
Michael Kickham

All Hallows College
Drumcondra
Oct 11th, '79

My Dear Parents,
I received your letter etc all right. I had a letter from Nicholas on Sunday last and I wrote to him a couple of days ago. He says that he is not a bit lonely.

I have not time to say any more but I hope you are all well.
Your affectionate son
Michael Kickham

All Hallows,
Jan 15th 1881

Dear Parents,

I would have written before now but I was waiting till I could see Charles, just to tell you how he is getting on. I went to see him on Thursday last, and I was not at all prepared to see him look so well as he did. He looked much stronger to my mind than ever I saw him look before, but he said he felt much better that day than he did for a long time.

I suppose you heard of the person he is stopping with. His name is James O'Connor he holds some office in the Irishman's office. He was in prison with Charles & they agree very well. His eyes are not at all as bad as you were telling me as he can read a little still, but he's afraid that they are failing very much.

There is scarcely a person about the country that he wasn't asking about, and he nearly knew as much about them as myself. He made me remain with him for dinner so that we were chatting for something about four hours and he made me promise that I would go out to see him again soon if possible. I was asking him would he wish ever to see Mullinahone again & he said that he would very much, but that he always shuts that out from his mind altogether, as he does not see any means of effecting it. If by any chance I go out to see him again I shall let you know more of him.

I was very sorry to hear that Maria Gleeson was so bad, I hope she has recovered. I got the rosary which we say every evening to be offered up for her recovery.

We had a very pleasant Xmas here this time considering the little means of enjoyment we have.

I hope you all enjoyed the season which is everywhere set apart to a certain extent for enjoyment.

Mike Egan was in to see me on St. Stephen's day. He said he spent a very pleasant Xmas and he desired to be remembered to all of you. We are altogether housed in here at present as there is about a foot of snow on the ground & it is freezing very hard.

When you are writing tell me all the news you can as the times are very dull here.

Hoping all are well.

I remain,

Your affect. Son

M C K

(be sure to write soon)

The Catholic hierarchy condemned the Fenians and the IRB for being a secret society and for the espousal of violence to pursue their aims. For this, they denied the sacraments to members. But Charles Kickham approached Archbishop Croke in Thurles pleading permission to have a confessor, which was granted. [6]

I was at home in Mullinahone in August 1882, when Charles died. There were reports of a huge cortege in Dublin as his coffin was brought to Kingsbridge railway station, to be transported to Mullinahone. The train stopped en route at Thurles and there was a hope that the coffin could repose in the Cathedral overnight. The Archbishop was away and the administrator of the diocese refused to allow it, because of Charles' Fenian and IRB activities. Afterwards the Archbishop wrote to Charles' brother Alexander offering condolences, in which he also said that if he had been there, he would have paid due honour to the remains.[7]

In Mullinahone, there was a very large crowd in attendance. The parish priest, an adversary of Charles and rabidly anti-Fenian, was away at the time, and both the church and the graveyard gates were locked. Someone managed to open the gates and the burial went ahead. As a clerical student, I had the honour of reciting the traditional *De Profundis* over the grave.[8]

Some said the parish priest was conveniently absent, but despite his strong anti-Fenian views, it's not clear that it was deliberate. He was often unwell and died less than a year later.

Too young

In 1882 my studies at All Hallows came to an end. I was not yet twenty one years, much too young to be ordained for which the minimum age was 24. But I was tonsured and admitted to Major Orders by Dr. Lynch, Archbishop of Toronto.

Father Fortune then called me to see him. "Michael", he said, "we have had a request from Bishop Redwood in Wellington, New

Zealand, to send curates to them. Bishop Redwood is of the Marist Order, as are most of the priests in the diocese. However, they have a scarcity of Marist priests and would like some secular Irish priests to help them out. I am thinking you would be ideal for New Zealand. The Marists are a French Order. You have an excellent command of French, so you would fit in very well.

"Furthermore because of your youth you cannot yet be ordained, so I am sending you to Le Grand Semenaire in Angers in France where you will study theology. In Le Grand Seminaire they follow the Suplicean way, which as you know, we have adapted here in All Hallows. Your ability in French will stand to you and during your time there you will become truly fluent. The experience there will be invaluable to you as a priest and missionary"

It was a statement of what was to happen next rather than a request as to whether I would like that. Still, I knew I was destined for the missions and the prospect of two years in Angers, followed by a missionary life in New Zealand, was appealing. At the time I thought nothing of the fact that I would be going to 'help out' the Marists. It would be some time before the import of this would become apparent.

I replied: "My mother's sister, my Aunt Annie Kirby, is living out there so I have heard quite a lot about it from her letters. I think I will like it."

I was looking forward to New Zealand.

When I got back to Mullinahone, Mother was delighted to hear I had completed my studies successfully, with a degree in Logic. "But what will you do now since you can't yet be ordained?" she asked, clearly worried that they might have sent me to All Hallows at too young an age. I explained that there was nothing to worry about. All Hallows planned that I would go to Le Grand Seminaire in Angers in France for two years for further study. I saw this as a bonus which other older seminarians who started with me in All Hallows, would not get to experience. I could see Mother's relief that sending me off while so young had worked out well after all. I also told her of the plan to send me to the missions in New Zealand. Mother was pleased that I would be going there, where her sister Annie was living.

Years later, when I returned to Mullinahone, she showed me a letter she had received from Melleray.[9]

Mt. Mellary Abbey,
March 10, 1878

Dear Catherine,

I had every reason to be vexed with you for not leaving Michael here another year. He required to be stronger before entering All Hallows, where even stronger full-grown young men sometimes break down and Fr. Ignatius who is one of the best-headed men in Ireland (at least I think so) fully agreed with me. Fr. Ignatius was vexed and no wonder for he was more anxious than you were to see Michael strong and healthy and he left nothing undone to make him so.

You may think it was for his own sake he wished Michael to remain another year, no, it was not but it was all for Michael's own sake and for the sake of his parents. Then had you left him here this year he would have more time to learn the piano as he would not require to study Latin, Greek or French which he knew sufficiently well.

His college course will be finished in his 20th year but he cannot be ordained 'til he's 24 years, however where will he spend his time during the few years that will intervene between the end of his college course and his ordination? I couldn't tell you all the objections Fr. Ignatius had to his being taken away so soon, it would take up too much space and time.

I hope however that what has been done will have good results.

You couldn't find in the wide world one who would give you better advice regarding Michael than Father Ignatius. Of course Father Ignatius felt he was not treated with consideration either by you or by the superior of All Hallows, at least I would so feel were I in his place.

I hope Michael's health continues good. As to his talents there can be no second opinion.

I hope Ned is well and his Mrs, also my esteemed friend Mr. Kickham. I heard nothing about the match until it was made. Mary Kenrick wrote to me about the matter a few days before the wedding. I think the new couple will be very happy, I'm sure they will and very prosperous. I was sorry to hear Ellen Kickham got very ill lately. I hope she is over the attack and well. I heard from Cappoquin today. It appears Sister Stanislas is now better than she has been for the last 7 years. The Curasilla people will be glad to hear this as will yourself and all true friends.

Don't show this letter to anyone but Mr. Kickham. I hope to write to you about Easter please God. Anne is very happy and evidently takes good care of her soul.

Ever yours
T. B. Laurence

Le Grand Séminaire Angers

Many of the French seminarians in Angers had been ordained and were being trained for life in the parish. Thus I got a level of practical training and preparedness for life in a parish, which I would not have received at All Hallows. This final part of the Suplician Way, the training after ordination, did not find its way into All Hallows.

One of my fellow students from Melleray, John Fogarty had been in Angers for three years. Paris with its Irish College was easily reached by train and we did get to visit a few times for a get-together with our compatriots. I met Patrick McKenna there and we became good friends. Like myself, he was due to be ordained in 1884.

Life in France was quite a change. Without French, I would have been isolated as very few of the French spoke any English.

I wrote to Bishop Redwood in Wellington to introduce myself and to express my gratitude at his accepting me for the New Zealand missions. He replied:

Jan 25ᵗʰ 1883

My Dear Mr. Kickham,
I have received your letter of the 5ᵗʰ of Nov. 1882. I hereby grant you in virtue of extraordinary faculties from the Holy See, dispensation for one year of your age.
I also would like the President of All Hallows to regulate the matter of your pairing.
Hoping your health is good.
I remain yours faithfully in JC

+ Francis Redwood

And I had to explain to my family that there were no Christmas cards to be had in France. I couldn't have them thinking I forgot, or worse, just didn't bother.

I also wrote to my cousin Tom to offer condolences on the death of his brother, Alexander Kickham.

My Dear Parents,

I wish you all a happy Christmas. I tried to get some Xmas cards to send Kattie & Tommy, but I have not been able. The French have no such custom & on that account they are not sold in the shops. However the intention is the most important point and they must only take the intention for the fact.

I think I was telling you last year about a remarkable tree that is not very far from here. The old story goes that when St. Patrick was passing through this part of France he had no means of crossing the river Loire at this point, so he took his cloak, placed it on the water & floated over to the other side. The night having set in, he laid himself down to sleep, stuck his stick in the ground and put his cloak on it to dry. When he awoke in the morning he found that his stick had taken root & though it was mid-winter it was in full flower. Ever since, the bush flowers twice a year, once at the same time with the others & again in winter. The strange thing is that at both sides of it there are bushes exactly alike but none of them has ever been noticed to flower and this has never been noticed to fail. When transplanted it does not flower. The parish is called after

St. Patrick & there is a church built there in his honour. It is about 40 miles from here. I went to see it last week but the flowers were almost all faded, however I saw some, it is just like any ordinary blackthorn.

I have just this moment received Kattie's letter, I'm very sorry to hear of poor Pat Byrne's death, it is dreadful to think how simply death comes on. It is a good thing the Mullinalough people are praying.

Twas a mean thing of Brown to refuse to let you meet the people at his house, knowing that you had nowhere else.

I wrote to Nick a few days ago, I hope he will get home.

Wishing you a very happy Xmas.

I remain, your fond son
    Michael

Wish all the cousins a merry Xmas & a happy New Year from me. Tom, Joe, Mrs K, Johnny Shea & family, the Clashmene family etc. I enclose a little branch of the tree. The couple of flowers I had are faded.

My Dear Tom,

You must have already applied to me the rule – the time of affliction proves friendship –; and I admit that I should have been more prompt in dropping you a few lines to express my sympathy for the loss of my cousin your dear brother. The letter announcing the sad news arrived here while I was on a pilgrimage to the grotto of Our Lady of Lourdes, and it was a consolation to me afterwards to think that I had not forgotten to implore the intercession of the Blessed Virgin in the place where she is more prodigal of her favours for him and my other friends.

I have also since my return got the prayers of the students offered up for the repose of his soul.

After all, Tom, is this not the real sympathy, what are words? The real sympathy is the sympathy which will serve best the lost one and console most the bereaved. A prayer to the Immaculate Mother of God begging her intercession for the repose of his soul would be more useful to him and as such more consoling to you than any amount of sincere words which proceed only from the lips.

I could not tell you the regret I felt when I heard of poor Alexander's death. As Charles was the pride of our name in a literary & political light, he procured it also a certain honour by his physical qualities. And to think that he so powerful in all his strength should be so quickly & easily overcome! Is that not a lesson!

Rejoice however that he has died such a happy death & that God although calling him away suddenly, has given him time & opportunity to prepare for that terrible moment. In praying God for the repose of his soul, we should beg of him for ourselves to be delivered from a sudden or improvided death. Before this letter will be arrived I shall be left here "en route" for Dublin. Pray for me as the point decisive of my future is at hand.

Your ever fond cousin
Michael C Kickham

Present my best respects to Joe and Mrs. Kenrick, hoping that themselves and family are well. Kindly tell them at home that I got their letter and will write probably tomorrow.

MK

Le Grand Séminaire,
May 26th 1884

My Dear Parents,

I received the P.O.O. [11] By the time you get this I shall probably be left France, at least I shall be on the borders of it. I leave here on Wednesday morning at 10 o'clock, leave Paris that same evening at 9 o'clock, arrive in London the evening after & in Dublin Friday evening at 8 o'clock, & on retreat the Sunday after. If you write Saturday I will get your letter on Sunday morning, but we get no other letters before the Sunday after. I am in a great hurry at present so you must excuse me.

Hoping you are all well.
Michael

Earlier that month, while still in Angers, I had been conferred *in absentia* with Sub-deaconate and Deaconate by the auxiliary Bishop of Dublin, Dr. Donnelly.[12] Also that month, the Holy See issued a dispensation to permit my ordination 17 months before my 24th birthday. [12]

All was now set for that final step to priesthood.

Ordination

I was back in Dublin just in time for the retreat. After this, I was ordained by the Bishop of Ardagh, Rev. Dr. Woodlock, on the 24th of June 1884, the feast of St John the Baptist.[13]

I went back to Mullinahone after this. Much to Father and Mother's delight and pride, I said my first mass there the following Sunday, 29th June.[14] The church, always full on a Sunday, was even more packed for my mass. All my family, cousins, friends, indeed nearly everyone in Mullinahone was there. It was a proud occasion for me.

My sister Kattie came up after the mass and gave me a big hug and said she was so proud. She was just sixteen at the time, but already very devout and pious. She was the apple of my eye. But over time I have to admit I became somewhat negligent in writing to her, and since coming to Buenos Ayres I never wrote at all, not to Kattie nor to anyone else for that matter.

I spent the month of July at home, meeting friends and family, being invited to their houses, all congratulating me and wishing me well, and very interested in knowing what the future held for me. I had been ordained for the New Zealand missions, but beyond that I really knew nothing.

7 – To the Antipodes

✳✳✳✳✳

O n Monday 1st of September 1884 I was in London ready to board the steamship *Garonne* bound for Melbourne. It was a strange feeling. Here I was, a young man from the small town of Mullinahone about to travel to the other side of the world. From autumn in this part of the world to spring down in New Zealand. I had feelings of apprehension and excitement, nervousness and joy, all rolled into one another. Soon all the more negative feelings faded and my confidence grew. I was looking forward to New Zealand.

Travelling with me from All Hallows were Richard Condon and Thomas Barlow for Sydney; Michael Gallagher for Brisbane; and for Melbourne, William Hartnett, Aeneas Hennessy, Michael Ryan and John Daly. Just myself for Wellington. They had all been together for the previous five years and knew each other well. I had spent the past two years in Angers, but before long of course I got to know them all and we cemented friendship.

I can remember the voyage so well.[1] We headed out of London, down the Thames estuary, through the English Channel, then

South towards the Mediterranean. I spent many hours at the railings, looking in amazement at the shorelines and landscapes we were passing, or at times just amazed at the endless expanse of ocean. The rock of Gibraltar was impressive as we entered the Mediterranean, a striking symbol of the Empire.

We sailed past the beautiful Isle of Capri as we headed into Naples for a brief stop to take on passengers. There were quite a few Italians emigrating to Australia, hoping to make a new life for themselves out there. Then on to Port Said where we commenced our passage through the Suez Canal.

I gazed wide-eyed at the hustle and bustle, and was overawed by the cacophony in the Egyptian city of Port Said. There were people everywhere, and you could hear the polished accents of the many well to do English walking around hither and thither. Rudyard Kipling once said *"If you truly wish to find someone you have known and who travels, there are two points on the globe you have but to sit and wait, sooner or later your man will come there: the docks of London, and Port Said"*, and it certainly seemed so.

We passed through the Suez Canal, a wonderful feat of modern engineering linking the Mediterranean and the Red Sea. At the other end of the canal, in the city of Suez, we stopped briefly. I had time to post a letter home.

Sailing down the Indian Ocean heading for Diego Garcia, we crossed from the northern to the southern hemisphere. With the sun ever higher in the sky, I was reminded of those lines by Samuel Taylor Coleridge from *The Rime of the Ancient Mariner*

> *The sun came up upon the left*
> *Out of the sea came he*
> *And he shone bright and in the night*
> *Went back into the sea*
> *Higher and higher every day*
> *Til over the mast at noon...*

During the day with the sun directly overhead the heat could be stifling, but often too there was a breeze which made it quite tolerable. The nights were warm and pleasant and we entertained ourselves.

Crossing the equator the whole ship was engaged in a light-hearted ritual to mark the event. There was an initiation rite for new sailors. It was deemed that by the time they reached the equator, they had proved themselves capable of enduring long and difficult sea voyages. The ceremony involved a visit from the god of the sea, King Neptune, his wife, Her Royal Highness Amphitrite, and their loyal assistant, Davey Jones.[2]

'Neptune' began by addressing the captain and crew and calling forth the first timers for induction. They had to sit in a chair above a pool in which 'angry bears' waited. They were then subjected to a 'medical' examination, shaved with wooden razors and dropped into the pool where the bears dunked them until they deemed them duly inducted into the kingdom of the deep. Each received a certificate recognising his new status as a Shellback.

It was all very entertaining for us passengers, not realising our own induction was yet to come. We were drenched with buckets of sea water being thrown over us, still entertaining and the wetting not unwelcome in the tropical heat.

On the 18th of October we arrived in Melbourne and I was able to go ashore for a few days. I met Father John Fitzgerald who was based at the Cathedral. John was from Mullinahone and had been ordained for Melbourne some fifteen years earlier. The next day, a Sunday, they were re-opening St. George's Church after renovations. Father Fitzgerald invited me to celebrate mass for the occasion.[3] There was a very large congregation present and I felt it a great honour.

A few days later I left my companions behind as I boarded for Wellington, arriving there on the 1st of November.

Wellington

Wellington, the capital city of New Zealand was a lot smaller than I had expected, nothing like the grand city that Dublin is. I think there were only around 25,000 people living there. I was brought to St. Mary's Cathedral and introduced to Bishop Redwood. The Bishop explained that he had installed a new marble altar and an organ. They were indeed very impressive. I remained in Wellington for several days, getting to know some of the local clergy and the city itself, with its fine imposing government buildings. [4]

As Father Fortune had told me in All Hallows, the diocese was indeed run by Marists, a French Order of Priests. Bishop Redwood was himself a Marist. He explained that there were not enough Marist priests to fulfil the needs of the diocese and its parishes, and that secular priests were being brought in from Ireland to assist them.

At the time I didn't think anything of the fact that we seculars were there to assist them. It seemed a sensible enough thing to do if there were not enough Marists. However, it would later become apparent that it wasn't quite so simple.

St. Mary's Cathedral,
Wellington . N.Z.
November 3rd 1884

My Dear Parents,

I am at last arrived at my destination safe & sound, if at all changed only fresher & stronger than when I set out. From the time I left home 'till I landed here was exactly two months. I left on the morning of the 1st September and only arrived here on the morning of the 1st November, so that considering that we kept going all that time we ought to be a pretty far distance by this time. Still strange to say I would think no more of going home again in the morning, if there were any necessity for it, than people would of going a twenty mile journey at home.

I forget where it was that I wrote to you from last, I suppose it was Suez. I would have written from Melbourne but as I was so near my destination I said it was as well wait & give you the final part in with the rest.

Taking the whole voyage all together I think we could not possibly have a finer one throughout. Except four or five days at different times that were pretty rough making nearly all the passengers and the other eight priests that were with me all seasick, there was nothing to complain of. During the whole time I never got sick for a moment. In fact I felt just as content there as if I was on land.

Our fellow passengers were mostly all very nice people, though except the priests, there were in the whole saloon only about four other Catholics. Once we got to know one another we began to enjoy ourselves very much. Mostly every evening that was fine we had the deck screened round and had a concert or a dance or some other amusement.

During the days there was always some game on foot either cricket or quoits or athletic sports etc. so that everybody was striving to make the time pass pleasantly for the others and everybody enjoyed himself.

From the time we left Suez we scarcely saw any land at all till we reached Adelaide. We got to run ashore there for a few hours and dined that evening with the bishop. I met Fr. John Healy from Glenashough and we went to see Dean Kennedy, John Egan's brother-in-law, where I met two or three who were at school with me in Melleray. Unluckily Fr. Mat. Kennedy was up the country so that I could not meet him.

At Melbourne where we had to change boat and bid good-bye to the "Garonne", we had three or four days delay waiting for the boat to take us to New Zealand. At Melbourne of course I felt quite at home as I knew about three quarters of the priests stationed in the city, at least about fifteen of them. Fr. John Fitzgerald is at present in the Cathedral there.

[The last part of this letter has not survived]

8 – New Zealand

I think back on my first two and a half years in New Zealand as my halcyon days. I was a young priest in a new country on the other side of the world, 12,000 miles from home. As a boy I could never have imagined this.

My life was now full of new experiences. The climate here was much warmer than back home although it did rain quite a bit. A few weeks after my arrival, I went to Napier, where I would spend the next two and a half years. I would assist the parish priest, Father Michael Grogan, who was a Marist. We got on well together and I think I gained his respect quite early on.

Napier was a large, sprawling parish. There were long journeys to visit the many scattered communities, some coastal, some inland. Waipawa was 25 or 30 miles south of Napier, and a distance in from the coast, while Wairoa, a coastal settlement, lay 75 miles north of Napier. The area to be covered stretched over 100 miles.

The journeys inland on horseback took me through some magnificent countryside, past mountains and across rivers. I sailed to the coastal settlements, with striking views to land.

In the beginning, I found it rather daunting heading off on my own to some of these communities. However, I soon gained confidence and familiarity and within a short period began to look forward to these trips.

I spent much time during the week teaching at St. Joseph's Marist school in Napier. Of course I also said Mass and administered the sacraments. Being among so many French Marists, I spoke French quite a bit. Father Fortune's comment that my time in Angers and my ability to speak French would be valuable, proved correct.

I was not yet two months in Napier when I took part in a Christmas prize-giving for outstanding pupils.[1] The principal, Father Sauzeau, was in the chair, with Father Grogan and myself on the platform. Together with other teachers, I donated a small prize.

Then on New Year's Day of 1885, there was the Jubilee celebration of another Marist father, Father Reignier, in the school hall.[2] I was the only non-Marist priest there.

In early 1885 I paid my first visit to Waipawa, a small settlement on the banks of the Waipawa river, in a very pretty setting. There is a fording point nearby where the ancient Māori trail between Manawatu Gorge and Hawke's Bay crosses the Waipawa River.

The priest there, Father Patrick Ahern, whom I knew from Mount Melleray and All Hallows, was called to Sydney, where his sister was seriously ill. I spent a month filling in for him .[3]

Learning of the ancient Māori trail set me thinking about the Māori people, the original New Zealanders. In Ireland I had never seen anyone other than white people. Here I sometimes found myself among the Māori who had a much darker skin colour. [4]

Some years before I arrived, the Northern Māori MP, Hone Mohi Tawhai, had told Parliament:

"I have heard of the people of Ireland, and the circumstances under which they were placed are very similar to the circumstances under which the Māoris are now placed. There were certain laws passed affecting their land, and it resulted in those people being deprived of their land. And now the same laws are being brought to bear upon us."

He went on to declare "I am an Irishman." Māori were remarkably well informed about the Irish situation and felt a bond with Ireland.

I recall thinking to myself: "New Zealand has its own parliament while Ireland must even now struggle to achieve Home Rule".

The 28th of September is the feast of St. Michael and was celebrated in the school each year.[5] There were two of us with the name Michael, Father Grogan and myself. Quite unexpectedly, less than a year after my arrival, I found we were both to be recipients of small presentations. The children presented a small musical interlude and afterwards I was presented with an illuminated address and a photograph album. This was my first time receiving a presentation, so it was quite special to me. I told the children I would hold it in especial esteem, and I did.

Like children everywhere, they asked if they could have a holiday in honour of the day. And as teachers everywhere would do, Father Grogan said yes, but only if they attended mass that morning. A good outcome for all.

The education delivered to the boys and girls at the Marist schools was second to none, much better than at the nearby state school.

St. Mary's
Napier
October 10th 1885

My Dear Parents,

Here I find myself again writing to you just at the last moment. It has already struck ten o'clock and I am tired after a pretty hard day's work. So as I must finish this to-night you need not expect much news. You will be glad to hear at any rate that I am still in the best of health never suffering in the slightest way and with every appearance that I am going to continue so. I feel confident that as long as I am left in Napier, I shall have nothing to complain of, as far as I can judge. How long they will leave me here is however another question. I am just 11 months here now and it seems as yesterday. It is not surprising how the months roll by particularly when you are kept a little busy.

Is Lory getting better, you never mentioned what was the matter with him, I suppose it is just a cold. I fear that he will sometime or other let himself be caught by it to such an extent, that it will end by his falling into consumption.

It would surprise you all the people that die of consumption out here, and still it is the best country perhaps in the world for consumptive people. Most of the young men however lead such a rough life, that it nearly always brings them to an early grave.

Winter and summer they sleep out on the mountain side in a tent made of canvas, lying on a little dried fern with just a couple of rugs around them. That is the way Pat Egan has been living for the past ten years, and strange to say they get so accustomed to that life that they do not like to leave it.

Five or six go together, they make their own bread and cook their own meat and that is all they have all the year round, dry bread and meat. The Sunday they spend in washing their shirts and stockings or stretching in their tents. A careful man working in the bush could easily put aside about £6 per month or £70 per year. Still strange to say you will not find one of these fellows worth a penny at the end of the year. One fortnight in town is enough to squander the whole year's earnings.

I wrote to Fr. Ignatius a short time ago and sent him a little cheque. Tommy seems to be getting on well. He has improved a great deal in writing. Let me know immediately what you have done about Kattie, and how she is getting on. The papers have not yet arrived giving the account of Charles' anniversary. I expect them this week.

When writing tell me how is the health of both of you, what way the business is going and all the news about everything.

Remember me to all the friends, I have not room to mention their names nor time either, as I must now go to bed.

Good night,
  M.C. Kickham

Wairoa on Hawkes Bay lies some 75 miles north of Napier along the coast, a whaling centre and an important area for the production of flax. I spent some time there ministering to the Catholic community. On the 24th of October 1885 I was treated to a birthday celebration, my 24th, by the local Catholic and Protestant communities. I was less than a year in New Zealand and this honour was totally unexpected. [6]

Mr. Moloney, a member of the community, spoke:
"Father Michael, you are a young, talented and zealous priest, and it's probable that you might not be left amongst us for too long. We therefore would like to take this opportunity of manifesting our esteem for you. Reverend Father, please accept this purse of sovereigns as a token of our appreciation of your diligent service to our community."

I was taken aback by the generosity. I replied:
"It is impossible for me to express the surprise I feel at this generosity by you, the people of Wairoa. Twelve months ago I had not yet arrived in New Zealand, and it is only some seven months since I visited Wairoa for the first time. I look in vain for anything I have done during that time to account for such generosity. There is only one explanation that I can see, and that is that the same bond that has always existed between the priest and his flock, between the Irish priest and his Irish congregation, is as strong here in this remote district of New Zealand as it is in the heart of Catholic Ireland, and it must needs show itself.
"I accept this gift as coming from Irish Catholic hearts to their soggarth aroon[7], and I only hope that in the future I might be able to repay you in the only way possible for me to repay you, by being even more zealous in attending to your spiritual wants."

There seemed to be celebrations and presentations at every opportunity. At the Christmas prize giving in the school, I received another beautifully illuminated address by Brother Joseph and a silver chalice from the pupils.

I replied:

"I am humbled by these presentations. In Brother Joseph's illuminated address, it is not just that I have been awarded this presentation, it is the honour of receiving such a work of art, for Brother Joseph is truly an artist of great skill. He is not just a skilled artist. He has opened the first branch of the Catholic Total Abstinence Society in New Zealand. I hope that ere long there will be many branches throughout the Colony.

"And now, the chalice: you can only imagine the joy it gives me to see the appreciation of the good Brothers and Sisters by parents and children. But I don't know what I have done to deserve this beautiful silver chalice which I will forever value. It will give me great pleasure on its first use to offer up the Holy Sacrifice of the Mass for the donors."

Napier,
Hawkes Bay. N.Z.
May 22nd 1886

My Dear Parents,

The mail before last, I wrote you a hurried note and intended writing again last mail, but just the day before the mail left I got an urgent telegram and had to start off at a few minutes' notice a long and rough journey.

To give you an idea of it, I will just tell you the circumstances. It was Good Friday just as I came down from the pulpit after preaching the passion sermon that I had to take a hurried bite, feed my horse and start off about midday. On the saddle before me I had to strap my overcoat. As I was going to attend a sick person I had to bring the Blessed Sacrament and Holy Oils, then in a satchel strapped on my back, I had a box of altar bread and a small bottle of wine, some vestments necessary for saying mass, my breviary and a few biscuits, making in all a pretty nice load.

In the first five hours of the journey, I travelled 30 miles and then it got pitch dark. I was of course all alone, mountains before and mountains behind, sometimes near the sea so that I could hear it beating on the rocks beneath. Sometimes some distance inland, no house within about twenty miles, except one or two shepherd huts. No sound of any description, it was the stillness of death.

For three hours it was dark, no moon or stars, no road, merely a track through the heather, like what you would see made by the sheep on the side of Slievenamon. I could not see the track from the horse's back, so I had to trust the horse though he had never done the journey before. In these three hours and a half, I only did ten miles. At about half past eight I got to a little house where I expected to get some food for man and horse, but the accommodation was more suitable for the horse than the man. The horse got a good feed of oats, but all I could muster was a bit of old black bread and a cup of black tea. With this refreshment we started again, but the moon had risen and was of great assistance in finding and keeping the track.

The next fifteen miles was similar up hill and down vale and that brought me at midnight to the bank of a big river. There is a man there usually, who ferries you across, both man and horse in a large boat, but the boat was locked and the man was not to be found. So I had to go to where the river was most shallow and get into it. Immediately I had to get almost on my knees on the saddle, as the water was more than half way up the horse's side and as it got deeper, I found it necessary to put my legs on the horse's back and kneel on the saddle and hold on by the pommel. It was in this position I reached the other side after getting only a few splashes of the water. I had then twenty miles to go, and got there at five o'clock, just at daybreak. You can imagine how tired myself and my horse were and with what pleasure I stretched my limbs after having prepared the person I went to see for death.

I am enclosing you a post-office order for £12 to help for the second half-year pension for Kattie. If you can spare her to have another year and I hope you can, I will try and provide for it. In my present position it is as much as I can do. You know that I would gladly do more if I could.

I am sorry to see the bad account of the past winter and spring. It seems to be spread all over the country. I trust that people will be able to pull through the bad times.

I hope you are all in good health. Lory seems to get on very slowly, if he is not cautious he will never get all right. Above all things let him never be out in the night air. From the experience I have had here I can see that it is the ruin of persons with weak lungs.

I had a letter from Aunt Anne yesterday, she is well, though not very stout, she is hardy and now that she does not work so hard she is getting on well.

Things are very dull here lately, people find it very hard to get on, and at the same time I must admit that the commonest labouring man here is as well fed as the most respectable farmers at home. Give my kindest regards to all the friends around and when writing give me an account of them all.

I am expecting a letter from Nicholas & get Tommy & Kattie to write when they are home for vacation.

Don't you mind Tommy's pension at Mellery, you try and keep him in clothes and books.

Good bye,
  Your fond son,
    Michael

My Dear Parents,

Kattie's letter just came to hand about a week ago and I am glad to see by it that you are all well though Lory's health might be better. I am really in a fix to know what to advise about Lory, it is more than probable that New Zealand's climate might serve him, that is, what we have here in Napier. But I don't see how I could do for him here till I have a house of my own to keep him in.

At the same time if the home climate does not suit him and the doctor advises change, well "in the name of God" let him come out here to see what it will result in. Of course there are many difficulties in the way, for the present at least. I cannot pay his passage. Then if he were not well on arriving I would have to pay his board in a hotel until I get a place of my own.

There is no doubt if he could struggle on for eight or ten months longer at home it would be much better. I think that by keeping himself well wrapped up in flannel and remaining completely indoors he would improve.

I was sorry to hear of the death of so many of the old people about. In the course of a few years. There will be very few of the old hands left. What with the bad weather and the bad times poor Ireland doesn't seem to prosper. They have got up a subscription list here to help the good causes at home. I think it will reach £120. We shall send it in a few days. The Irish here are a small minority.

What have you done about Kattie's going back, I was very much pleased with the letter she sent me. Indeed I did not dream of her being able to do so well. I shall try to send a few pounds to you next mail. It is a pity if you haven't been able to give her another year. If you can spare her at all, I will try to help to make the pension all right until next summer.

I am glad to hear that Nicholas was home and that he is getting on well. I will write to him probably next mail. I assure you it is not always easy to find time to write when out here.

I am sending you two papers with an account of a dinner and concert on them.

Anything that I should ever send home or do for Kattie or Tom, it is better not speak of it.

With fondest love to you all,

I remain your fond son,

Michael.

A Parish Priest

In early 1887 I got word that I was to be made Parish Priest of Lyttelton on South Island. I would now have sole charge of a parish and no longer be living in a community of Marist fathers. I relished the prospect, being at once excited and apprehensive.

I received presentations from the school pupils: a missal from the boys at the Marist Brother's School; and a beautifully embroidered alb from the girls of the Convent School. The next evening, there was a presentation and send off by fellow priests and parishioners, chaired by Father Grogan, whom I had been assisting.[8] He spoke:

"Today we bid farewell to Father Kickham, an excellent priest who is departing from us. Personally, I have every reason to regret this as we have laboured together in the field for over two years. I have watched you carefully, Father Michael, and I have found your life a sterling one in every respect. You have been a faithful priest, attentive to your duties, which you have performed with gentlemanliness, and a willing earnestness. His Lordship has looked all over his diocese for one to fill a vacancy, and his choice has fallen upon you, whom we love. It is a great thing to be a parish priest, to have charge of the souls of a whole district, and that is the charge that has fallen upon you, Father Michael."

Mr. Cullen, a parishioner, continued:

"Dear and Reverend Father, we, the Catholics of Napier, while most cordially congratulating you upon your promotion to the charge of the parish of Lyttelton, desire to express the regret which we feel at your departure from our midst. We desire to mark our grateful recognition of the zeal, prudence, and devotedness with which you have discharged your duties as a priest, and our appreciation of those private virtues

which have endeared you in a special sense to every class of your faithful and ever loving people. It has indeed been a cause of pleasure to us to perceive that whilst as a faithful priest you have given your just care to the duties of your sacred calling, as an Irishman you have never forgotten that your country's claims were only second to those of the Church. Your genuine, warm hearted patriotism, and the encouragement you have given to movements having for their object the welfare of our Fatherland, have closely united you to us whose hearts share your feelings of patriotic devotedness to Ireland. We beg you to accept the accompanying purse of sovereigns."

I responded, filled with emotion:

"Most of you have, as exiles forced or voluntary, already felt the pangs of leaving a good father or mother, and for that reason you can understand the trying position in which you have placed me, when I have to meet all of you whom I might call brothers, to bid you a public farewell. I can safely say that there are no circumstances which would cause me more pain and regret than what I feel at this moment, in having to bid good-by to all the friends I see around me. You have given me a token, as you said, of the esteem and regard in which you hold me. But I have a still more pleasant token of your esteem and regard in the kindness and sympathy expressed in your faces gathered here around me. I must say that the past two years and four months, during which time I have been amongst you, has been a time of happiness and pleasure. After the discharge of my sacred duties as a priest, there is nothing that would give me greater satisfaction than to assist the cause which you all have so much at heart — the cause of poor old Ireland. I also wish to thank all those who, though not members of our Catholic congregation, and whom I have met in the discharge of my duties, without exception have always been very courteous towards me. I wish you all a hearty farewell and good-bye."

After this, Mr. Hornsby, a Protestant, stood up. He had chaired a meeting on Home Rule some months previously where he said he was the only person present who was not an Irishman, but that he had studied the question of justice to Ireland and wished to see the implementation of Gladstone's proposal of Home Rule for Ireland. [9] He sympathised with the struggles that Irishmen would make until they succeeded in their aims.

> *"I would like to say a few words as an outsider. I am not a member of your congregation, and I am not an Irishman, but I have very much pleasure in saying that in Rev. Father Kickham I believe that both Catholics and Irishmen in this town and district are losing a warm-hearted friend. On behalf of all those who do not belong to the Catholic congregation, I wish you good-bye and God speed."*

Reflecting back on my time in Napier, I feel all in all it was good. The experience of living in a new country and facing many new challenges were all very exciting. I got to know and understand my parishioners, and managed to earn their respect – their kind words certainly suggested that, and I hope I am not guilty of self indulgence in relaying their many praises.

It was tiring enough getting around to the outlying communities but there were rewards from these visits. I also got to see how some of the pioneers lived their Spartan lives and in the process make good money but blow it all away in a couple of weeks in town.

I got on well with the many Marists, however I became aware that my prospects were limited as a secular priest. My appointment as Parish Priest to Lyttelton gave me some hope.

The appointment of a Bishop to Christchurch was awaited. There was considerable pressure from both Bishop Moran in Dunedin and Cardinal Moran (no relation) in Sydney for the new Bishop to be from the ranks of secular priests. Rumours suggested otherwise, that a Marist would be appointed. Time would tell.

Next morning, while waiting to board the steamship Tarawera for Lyttelton, I saw a rather puzzling letter in the New Zealand Daily Telegraph:

Sir,

I am very loath indeed to take up the space of your valuable columns but I am very anxious to learn with many others by what right a Mr Hornsby took upon himself to attend and address a meeting as the representative of the Protestant bodies in Napier in giving a farewell to the Reverend Father Kickham on leaving this place. I doubt very much whether Mr Hornsby ever saw or spoke to the Reverend Father until that evening. There are plenty of old Protestants in Napier who have known Father Kickham for a long period, and who would have been only too glad to have said a word of praise in his favour. It was thought by many of us that, as it was a meeting purely Catholic, saying goodbye to their pastor, that it would have been an intrusion on our part to be there, but when an utter stranger to the people and the place has the audacity to get up unasked and uninvited and speak in the name of the whole of the Protestant Communities of this place, it is sheer gross impertinence.

Can you not see, Sir, what a painful position it must have put the Reverend Father in; here is an utter stranger to himself and the people posing as the representative of about 7000 people of different creeds. Why, Sir, it is the grossest piece of impertinence I ever heard of. I trust that Father Kickham will give us the credit when I say that we deplore the circumstances altogether, and I have no doubt that he takes the good wishes and affectionate regards of all those Protestants that have known him here and trust that he will live long to continue and carry out that which he has so nobly devoted his life to.

I am etc,
A Protestant

I wondered what prompted that letter. I certainly had not felt I was put in *"a painful position"*. I had in fact met Mr. Hornsby before.

Yet it was nice to read that I had all the good wishes and affectionate regards of the many Protestants in the community that knew me.

Lyttelton

Lyttelton is the harbour for Christchurch on the South Island, and I was to have full charge of the parish. I arrived into a small port town on the 8th of March and was met by Father Ginaty, the parish priest in Christchurch. He showed me around and introduced me to the nuns and brothers at the school, who had arranged accommodation for me.

I soon came to realise that having sole charge of the parish was rather less impressive than I had imagined. The parish was very spread-out and it was difficult to cover its full extent. In reality I should have had an assistant. The population of less than 500 was barely able to support me, but I was determined to succeed.

I began to get a stronger sense here that the Marist priests did not consider us seculars their equals. They regarded us as mere assistants who were only there to help them out. Many Irish seculars had charge of the more remote and difficult parishes, including in the gold mining area on the west coast. Conditions there were tough and income was meagre enough. There might have been gold there but most who came to make their fortunes saw little of it.

The divide between us seculars and Marists wasn't helped by news that the Bishop of the new diocese of Christchurch was to be a Marist and an Englishman at that. So the rumours were well founded. I wondered how all this would play out.

I was just a few months in Lyttelton, when on the 26th of July 1887, Dr. John Joseph Grimes SM, a Marist, was consecrated Bishop of Christchurch.[10] He wasn't actually in New Zealand at the time: it would be several months before he arrived.

Meanwhile, I had to see to my own needs and set about looking for a parish house to live in. I was supported in this by the parishioners of Lyttelton. Few enough as there were, they rowed in with enthusiasm. Within a few months we found one and managed to get it at a bargain price.

My Dear Parents,

I have before me two unfinished letters, both of which were begun for the two Frisco mails which left here these past two months. We are in the midst of the cold weather here, today it is miserable almost as cold and dreary as your winter at home. We had some snow this morning and now it has changed to sleet and cold rain. You would be astonished at the difference of climate between here and Napier, almost the same difference as between the south of Ireland and the south of France.

When out on the hills about a fortnight ago, on the monthly trip that I make to a place called Akaroa, I was over many hills that are covered with snow during a great part of the winter. This monthly visit is the hardest part of my work here. On an average I have to ride close to 200 miles during the five or six days I am out, some days riding 60 miles and carrying a number of things besides on the saddle.

Some parts of the roads are good, others very bad. In the wintertime particularly there are many places impassable and some where you have to wade half a mile through water from two to three feet deep. I have a good horse, one I got from Aunt Anne. He is just the sort that suits me, strong and active. He thinks nothing of bringing me from Akaroa (60 miles) in 8 hours.

I don't know if I wrote to you since I purchased my new house. It is a splendid building, large, handsome and solid, and better than all comparatively cheap, though I daresay you would call it dear. It is a two story house having nine rooms, with pantry, scullery, wash-house etc. besides and about a quarter acre of a garden, beautifully laid out. The building alone cost £1,400 and there must have been about £100 spent on the garden. So that it was not very dear when we got the whole thing for £725. The furniture and the necessary changes, deeds etc. cost about £100 more, and as we have £300 on hand that will leave a debt of about £500 on it, which we hope to be able to pay in about two years. I am now arranging to get the nuns to take charge of our school in which we have some 70 children and when that will be completed, then all the wants of the parish will be supplied. All that will remain after that will be to raise the money to pay off our debts, which considering the bad times, the smallness of our congregation and their poverty will be no easy matter.

We have not more than 80 families in the town or about 400 people and they are all depending on their days' wages. There are nearly as many scattered over the peninsula as we have in the town, but they are not much good to support the church though they are for the most part very comfortable. They are a motley crowd from all nations. One Sunday lately I met ten or twelve of them after mass and there were among them 1 Italian, 2 Frenchmen, 1 Pole, 1 Portuguese, 1 from the island of Madeira, 1 German, 2 colonials and an Irishman and a half. In my district here I believe you could find a person form every nation under the sun. We have Russians, Greeks, Swedes, Norwegians, Danes Turks, Swiss, Austrians, Americans, Chinese, Arabs, Syrians, etc. etc. So you see what a strange part of the world this is.

There is a good deal of excitement here about the appointment of our new Bishop for Christchurch. He is it seems an Englishman though it seems one of his parents is Irish. His sympathies are I believe English. The people are very much put out over his appointment. It seems the English faction at home had something to do with his appointment.

I must send some money to Fr. Ignatius in a few days, though I must say that since I came here I cannot spare very much. All the parishes here are poor, at least those parishes set apart for the secular priests. The Marist Fathers have those that are worth anything, and as we consider that an injustice, it is more than probable that a large number of our body will leave the diocese before very long. However nothing will be done for some few months yet. I trust you are all well & strong so that you are able to keep things going, which is not too bad in these times.

Your fond son,
Michael

I seemed forever to be battling with postal deadlines. Sometimes the letters would go via Australia and Suez, sometimes they would go via the F'risco service, across the Pacific to San Francisco, across America by train and onwards across the Atlantic.

Disaffection with Marists

Late in 1887 I met Father James O'Donnell. He had also been in Melleray and All Hallows, but as he was four or five years older than me, I hadn't known him well. James was living in the Marist house in Christchurch. We were both involved in St. Joseph's school in Lyttelton, where I was chairman. In December we set exams for the boys. The top performers would receive prizes.

The previous month, Archbishop Redwood (acting for Bishop Grimes pending the new Bishop's arrival in New Zealand) had removed James from his position as parish priest of Ahaura on the west coast and brought him back as curate in Christchurch.[11] James told me his removal was because he signed an address to Bishop Moran in Dunedin, a secular bishop, complaining about the difficulties attached to working as a priest under the Marists.

He also said the Archbishop had told him his career would be 'blasted' in Wellington and Christchurch, and he was offered permission to leave New Zealand. He refused to go, but told the Archbishop he wouldn't trouble him for long.

Father O'Donnell was invited back to Ahuara for a presentation by the parishioners, an indication of the esteem in which they held him. He was subsequently given control of the area of Darfield, some 25 miles from Christchurch. Clearly, he also served the people of Darfield well: his parishioners noted the hardship of getting to the remoter communities on horseback, so they raised funds to buy him a trap and harness. [12]

"Michael," he said, "life is becoming unbearable for us secular priests, with the way the Marists carry on. I'm fed up of hearing we are only here to assist them. They give us the poor and more remote parishes while they take all the plum appointments. We addressed some concerns to Bishop Redwood and indeed it did seem we were making some headway for a time. He sanctioned an annual church gate collection to fund a retirement home for secular priests. But when one Marist objected, he reneged saying that it could only proceed if all parishes were in agreement. That means that each and every Marist priest has a veto on anything we want to do. This is so unjust. We have to take this further."

"In Napier, my appointment was as assistant to Father Grogan, and in truth I did not take much note of being just an assistant," I replied. "After all, it was my first assignment. But at the same time it became clear to me that as a secular, my prospects would be limited. Then my appointment to Lyttelton raised my spirits – I would have sole charge of my own parish. However, it is not quite what I expected. I may have full responsibility for the parish, but it has a very small Catholic population, dispersed widely. As a result I spend a lot of time each month just to get around to the outlying communities. Being on the move so much is very tiring and places to eat and stay are often quite wretched. Most of my collection seems to go on accommodation, subsistence and feeding my horse. Not much left for myself.

"However, despite the hardship, I enjoy meeting and working with the parishioners. But hearing Marist priests say to me that we are only here to assist them is very demeaning and disheartening. We would benefit from more respect and better conditions but I don't see any evidence the Marists have any appreciation of the harm they are doing. Who do we appeal to? Cardinal Moran in Sydney? I was in both Dunedin and Wellington for his visit to New Zealand last year. He seems a good man."

Perhaps I should clarify, there were two senior churchmen by the name of Moran: Bishop Moran in Dunedin and Cardinal Moran (not related) in Sydney.

James replied:

"Cardinal Moran is a great man, very supportive of the Irish secular priests. But try as he did, he was unable to secure a secular diocese in Christchurch. No, we have to go higher."

"Are you suggesting we should appeal to the Pope himself?"

"Yes I am. Will you support me?"

This was quite a prospect. Could we really do this? What would be the implications for our ministry if we were seen to go over the head of our Bishop? It seemed a very dramatic step to take. I thought for some time before replying: "Yes James, you can count on me."

And thus was put in train our petition to Pope Leo XIII. We worked on it over many months, drafting and re-drafting. We approached other Irish secular priests for their support. We tried to avoid any Marists or the Bishop himself getting word of what we were doing, even to the extent of not approaching a few of the Irish seculars we felt would not support us.

All the while we tended to our regular parish affairs – saying mass, hearing confessions, preparing children for communion and confirmation, performing weddings and funerals, visiting the remote communities, as well as teaching in the school.

New Bishop arrives

In the midst of all this, in February 1888, Bishop Grimes arrived in Christchurch.[13] He travelled by ship to Lyttelton, the port for Christchurch, accompanied by Archbishop Redwood of Wellington and Metropolitan for New Zealand. They went immediately to St. Joseph's Church. The new Bishop said the first mass at 9 am, followed by a second mass at 9.30 celebrated by the Archbishop.

Father Chervier and myself prepared a welcoming address for the new Bishop. As Parish Priest, they were my guests for the day and I showed them around the town. The Nuns arranged a lunch fit for the occasion. That afternoon, a special train was put on to take the party to Christchurch, after which I could relax. I hadn't been over enthused by the appointment of a Marist and an Englishman as my Bishop, yet he seemed pleasant and courteous that day. I deferred judgement for the time being.

Petition to Pope

We seculars definitely had a raw deal from the Marists. We wrote what transpired to be a very long petition[14] to Pope Leo XIII, setting out our many grievances:

> *To be presented under the patronage and the favour of The most Eminent and Illustrious Cardinal Simeoni, Prefect of the holy congregation for Propaganda, To our most holy Father in God, Pope Leo XIII Bishop of Rome and Vicar of Jesus Christ, Successor of St. Peter, Prince of the Apostles, Supreme Pontiff of the Universal Church.*
>
> *The Humble Petition of the undersigned ... most submissively and respectfully shewith:*
>
> *That we have been the subject of discrimination;*
>
> *That Propaganda Fide in Rome must have been deceived when granting the Marists exclusive rights to certain districts;*
>
> *That we have complained to Bishop Redwood, but despite promises, received no reply;*
>
> *That the Marists have all the best missions while the seculars have the poor ones, made worse by how extensive they are geographically, requiring much travelling and having to expend most of the collection money on travel and subsistence;*
>
> *That, while the Marists have their own retirement home, there is no provision for retiring, infirm or unwell secular priests;*
>
> *That the Marist priests adopt a superior air saying the secular priests are only there to help them;*
>
> *That we have no fair and independent advocate vis-a-vis Marists because both the Archbishop of Wellington (now Metropolitan) and the*

Bishop of Christchurch are Marists and as such presumably prejudiced against the secular priests

That the secular priests have … hitherto refrained from making an appeal to the Holy See, for the following reasons, to with:

Firstly: … we looked upon an appeal to Rome as an extreme proceeding

Secondly: … making an appeal to the Holy See would provoke much more ill feeling …

Thirdly: we greatly dreaded … the consequences of incurring our Bishop's … extreme displeasure, which … deters several of us from signing this Petition and those who sign it will do so with sorrow and trepidation.

That … we turn our eyes and our hearts imploringly towards Apostolic Rome and place all the hope that remains to us in the highest and last Tribunal on Earth. Woe betide us if we are doomed to failure and disappointment. Our condition will be if possible much worse than before.

We come to the feet of Your Holiness to suggest …the only remedy that seems to us at once simple, practical and effective … :

That all the Marist priests are sent to one diocese, Wellington or Christchurch as they prefer and that they have the complete, total, exclusive and perpetual possession of all the missions and properties of the diocese they choose, if that pleases the Holy See and that all secular priests are placed in the other diocese which we ask Your Holiness to secularise and that they are treated on their merit like all other missionaries of good reputation and ability.

That … we strive to imitate the example of our father Abraham … directed at ending the quarrels that arose between his herdsmen and those of his nephew Lot.

"I pray thee let there be no strife between me and thee, and between my herdsmen and your herdsmen, for we are brothers. Behold the whole land before you, separate yourself from me I pray you. If you will go to the left hand, then I will go to the right. If you choose the right, I will go left." Gen XIII, 8 and 9.

*If unfortunately our humble proposition cannot be executed, we
humbly beg your holiness to inform His Excellency Monsignor the
Archbishop of Wellington and His Excellency Monsignor Grimes
Bishop of Christchurch that they should ... agree to grant us
testimonial letters so that we can have the right to be able to seek
elsewhere the justice they have continuously refused us here.*

*May the decision on our petition be favourable but if not we pray
that it may please Your Holiness to afford us an apostolic blessing.*

*We sign as the most humble and obedient servants, children in need
and pleading petitioners to Your Holiness:*

Dated Festival of St Thomas Aquinas, 1888

The festival of St. Thomas Aquinas was on the 7th of March.

Eighteen secular priests in Christchurch and Wellington signed.
A few refused to sign. There was another few we did not approach
as we felt they would not be happy with the petition.

I thought it presented our grievances in a clear and
unambiguous way. Surely they must see that in Rome?

St. Patricks Day 1888

My troubles began a month later. The new Bishop presided at a
gathering for St. Patricks Day in Christchurch. Everything started
off well enough with the Bishop proposing formal toasts to 'The
Pope', 'The Queen' and 'The Governor'. Father Smythe proposed
'The Day We Celebrate', responded to by Mr. Loughman. Mr.
Lonergan proposed a toast to 'Charles Stuart Parnell and the Home
Rule Party' and I responded: [15]

*"I need scarcely say that I am extremely pleased to have the
opportunity to respond to Mr. Lonergan's Toast, indeed it is a privilege
to respond to a Toast of Parnell and the Home Rule Party, and I am
proud to do so.*

"I do not wish to slight Mr. Parnell in any way when I say that the foremost point here is not Mr. Parnell himself, but rather the matter which he represents, Home Rule. Mr. Parnell is an illustrious man and he has illustrious followers. His name is known throughout the world because of the way he advocates for Ireland. There are other noble men whom I would like to suggest are partners in the work of Mr. Parnell, men who throughout this century have worked for the same cause. In this, Daniel O'Connell is the first that comes to mind. That name should not be forgotten. Neither should the names of Young Irelanders Gavin Duffy and Thomas Davis.

"I would also like to call to mind those patriotic but at present so much despised men who have served their country, even if they have not done so wisely, men who work in a body condemned by the Church. I am referring to the Fenians. They know they are morally wrong, still they are true to the cause. They are animated by one motive only: love of their country.

"But there is no one who would not feel a surge of pride suffuse him at the mention of the name Charles Stuart Parnell. He found Ireland in a state of oppression. By his own power and that of his patriotic band he has raised Ireland to the feeling that she is a power in the land and she has a cause which is bound to triumph. We should feel proud at the bare mention of his name. Nor should we forget his followers such as Thomas Sexton, T.P. O'Connell, William O'Brien, James Dillon and others in their strong pursuit of Home Rule.

"There are many others who have been prominent in the struggle and I fully agree with Mr. Nolan when he said that it would be showing appreciation of their services if they were to receive financial help. It would be well if Irish people here gave more practical assistance to the Home Rule movement than merely drinking the health of the Irish Party.

"Let us expect that in time we will no longer toast Our Home Rule Party, rather the Irish Parliament. Let us hope that before long we will celebrate St. Patrick's Day when the toast of the evening will be "to Ireland a Nation".

Later there were many calls for Father O'Donnell to speak too, but the Bishop wouldn't have it. The New Zealand Tablet reported that it was indeed a disappointment not to hear him:

Many people could not readily reconcile themselves to the loss which they sustained in not hearing Father O'Donnell upon a subject so congenial to him as one of the patriotic toasts would have been.

The Tablet commented very favourably on my speech:

The speeches were all good but once and only once during the evening was the assemblage electrified and that was by Father Kickham.

Father Kickham is a genuine Irish orator, something of the type of the brilliant Thomas Francis Meagher, whom he resembles in no slight degree. Father Kickham possesses a fine, clear, ringing voice, a manly bearing, and every word which he uttered in reference to Charles Stewart Parnell, and the men who in all times have sought to win freedom for Ireland, came straight from his heart, and went to the hearts of his hearers, causing the blood to flow quicker and hearts to beat faster.

There was no uncertain sound of half hearted lukewarm tone about Father Kickham's address. Every Irishman who ever strove to free his country from her long bondage, evidently has a claim upon Father Kickham's gratitude, and came in for a good word. At the conclusion of Father Kickham's brilliant, manly, straight-out speech, the room rang with the most genuine outburst of applause elicited by any speech during the evening and enthusiastic cheers were given for Charles Stewart Parnell.[15]

Clash with Bishop

However, my worst fears were realised. The Bishop was not pleased with my speech. He called me to provide an explanation. "Father Kickham, at the St. Patrick's Day festivities you praised members of a body condemned by the Church. You named the Fenians. Clearly you know that that organisation is a secret society and promotes violent means to achieve their ends. That is why they have been condemned by the Church and why what you said was unacceptable. I cannot accept and condone a priest of my diocese speaking out like this. At mass next Sunday I want you to publicly apologise for what you said."

I began to feel quite annoyed, but I kept control and replied calmly: "Your Lordship, please hear me out. Firstly, let me say that I am unashamedly in favour of Home Rule. I do not advocate violence in pursuit of political goals and have never done so. Secondly, while I named the Fenians, I made it quite clear that they are morally wrong and that they know this. I also made it clear that they were a body condemned by the Church.

"I should add that my cousin Charles, deceased these past five years, was a founding member of the Fenians, something that is well known here by many. It would have seemed strange if I had not made some reference. But I was clear in stressing the error of their ways. I do not see that there is anything I said for which I should apologise, and indeed the very fact of making such a public apology would imply that I believed I had done wrong. With the greatest respect I would ask that you not insist on this."

My reply seemed to have the desired effect. But then, the following Sunday Dr. Grimes, from the altar, said that at first he contemplated asking me to make a public apology for the reference in my speech to a certain organisation.[16] He then went on to say that he would not pursue that course because he was satisfied with my explanations.

I was incensed. If he was satisfied with my explanations, why did he feel it necessary to publicly humiliate me? I felt it was going to be difficult for me to live in this environment and I resolved to see whether I could leave the diocese. I was aware that I had made a commitment when coming here, but surely there must be some recognition of extenuating circumstances?

The Tablet seemed bewildered at the Bishop's pronouncement:

But I can most emphatically say that no one to whom I have spoken who was present at the banquet that night in the least misunderstood his remarks or for a moment imagined that he intended in any way to eulogize the society which the Church had censured.

Canterbury Literary Society

Easter Monday that year we had the annual picnic of the Canterbury Catholic Literary Society, which was held on Mr. Gardener's estate. [17] The estate is very prettily located, close to the coast and surrounded by woodland, with hills behind. I made my way there by sea thanks to a kind fisherman who brought me over in his boat. It was a very pleasant day, with a marquee set up for food and beverages and a game of cricket on the lawn.

The Society ran a regular programme of readings, discussions and debates covering a wide range of topics, making a valuable contribution to the Catholic community and I enjoyed attending from time to time. It was for the most part a lay Catholic affair, but both Secular and Marist priests would attend from time to time, as would the Bishop. Of course Secular priests and Marists were respectful to one another on those occasions.

But as time went on, the chasm between us Seculars and the Marist fathers became more apparent to me and I was not happy. When I heard my brother Tommy might have a vocation, I felt I should warn him about what was happening here.

Lyttelton,
18ᵗʰ April 1888

My Dear Parents

You spoke about advising Tommy as to the selection of New Zealand for his future home. If you think he has a vocation and means to study for the priesthood, I certainly advise him for the present to bind himself to no bishop least of all to any in New Zealand. Ecclesiastical affairs here are not going quite smoothly, for the present things are rather upset. The position of the Irish secular priests in Christchurch and Wellington dioceses is by no means an enviable one and it is quite possible that before twelve months many of us may select some other diocese in which to labour. The matter is at present before the Holy See at Rome and we shall act according to the advice we get from there.

This country is at present in the state of great depression, thousands are leaving it for the other colonies and although it certainly has a great future before it, for many years it will make little progress. This province of Canterbury is at present the most depressed though for many years it has been the most flourishing.

There are many people here who are almost starving, but then it is in a great measure owing to their improvidence. They never think of depriving themselves of anything as long as they have food, money or credit. A man came to me a short time ago and said that he had not a morsel of food in the house or any means of getting it and himself and family were in absolute want, so I gave him an order to a grocer to give him a few shillings worth and advised him to make it go as far as possible.

Now what do you think he bought? He had sardines as next day was Friday, some salad oil, a bottle of Worcester sauce and a lot of other trifles so that the 8s worth he got only did him to the next day or altogether a day and a half. There is as much wasted in some workmen's houses as would keep a family at home and yet these people that waste like that complain loudly that they are in a state of poverty.

I am enclosing a photograph of Lyttelton, you will see what it is like. Everybody lives on the shipping. We have only about 400 Catholics all told in the town and not more than 200 adults. There is sitting room for only 120 in our little church so that you may see that Lyttelton is not of extraordinary importance. In the country district which is very large, about 80 miles long and about 40 miles wide, there are about 200 to 250 Catholics and I spend a week of each month going from place to place among them teaching the children catechism etc. It is very disagreeable to have to be continually on the move and above all to have often wretched places in which to eat and sleep.

I have no letter from Aunt Annie lately but I fear it is my own fault as I have not written for some time. During the past few months I may say I have written to no one. I have had to dispose of the horse she gave me as he turned out rather nasty. Twice he put me clean out of the saddle over his head into a pool of water. Horses here have a very impolite way of asking the riders to dismount. They get their head between their legs and by jumping and writhing and twisting their bodies they will get the very best riders off. I have known some of them to get the saddles off without even breaking the girths, but work it over their head and foremost feet. I have not sold my horse yet, he is on grass, but I will sell him soon, I expect about £17 or £18 for him.

I am sending you a couple of copies of the Tablet, you will see an account of our St Patrick's Day banquet at Christchurch at which I spoke.

The Bishop presided, but as he is not an Irishman, and even has not much sympathy for Ireland, he threw a damper on the whole meeting. He was not pleased with my remarks though I think he was the only one in the room who was not. He did not wish any of the young Irish priests to speak and though Fr. O'Donnell was called for over and over again, he would not allow him to speak because, he said, it was too late. I fear that what the Tablet said was true, he was sent out by the Duke of Norfolk's crowd in order to lessen the help to be given to the cause at home by the Irish people out here.

I shall be very busy now for two months preparing the children throughout the district for confirmation. Of course I have to do everything myself. For though there might be enough work for another priest it would not support two, in fact it cannot well support one.

Write soon and give me all the news you can. I get the papers you send regularly. Hoping to hear soon and that you are all well.

Your fond son
Michael C K

Duke of Norfolk's Crowd

Many English Catholics thought that Irish nationalism was revolutionary and abhorrent. They were not happy that priests and bishops in Ireland supported Home Rule. It was not enough for the hierarchy to speak out against violence, they wanted to see opposition to Home Rule. The Duke of Norfolk and others, with their connections in Rome, tried to influence the selection of priests and bishops in Ireland.[18] In New Zealand too, it seemed.

O'Connor Testimonial

In June we had the presentation of the O'Connor Testimonial. I had to ride sixty miles that day in order to do honour to Mr. O'Connor. I proposed "The National League":

> "It's not yet 10 years since 20,000 tenant farmers came together in Claremorris, demanding 'The Land of Ireland for the People of Ireland'. This was the start of the National Land League and the struggle for the three Fs – Fair Rent, Fixity of Tenure and Free Sale. I would remind you all of how the people of Ireland had become so accustomed to persecution that they had lost all heart till the advent of the League. But the League has caused the buoyant spirits, so characteristic of us Irish, to revive. Three years ago, the Ashburton Act set up a £5 million fund and any tenant wanting to buy land can now do so. Tenants can take a loan from the government and pay it back in monthly instalments over 48 years. When The National Land League was suppressed, Charles Parnell established The National League with the added commitment to press for Home Rule. By means of the League, the social position of the people of Ireland has been raised, and many other good influences have come from it. I would especially like to compliment Michael Davitt for his patriotism and commitment to the Irish Cause. The struggle will continue until Ireland and the Irish people control their own destiny." [19]

Official visit of Bishop

That same month, Bishop Grimes made his first formal visit to Lyttelton (his stopover in Lyttelton on his arrival at Christchurch didn't constitute a formal visit to the port).[20] I was responsible for making the various arrangements. Despite our clash after St. Patrick's Day, I continued to deal politely with him, as did he with me.

Lyttelton,
June 6th 1888

To The Right Rev. Dr Grimes SM

My lord

On Monday last I intended calling on you but found you had left for the south just before I arrived at the presbytery. The principal object of my visit was to know if the time we have arranged for your visit to Lyttelton would meet your wishes, viz by the train leaving Christchurch at 5.30 pm on Saturday June 16th. That will be the most convenient time for the people here, as the congregation here is made up for the most part of the working class who finish work a little earlier than usual on the Saturday evenings.

I would also be glad if you could defer your visit to Akaroa for some time so that I might arrange for a few days mission there to prepare them for confirmation. The great majority of those to be confirmed are adults, some of whom, living a distance from the church, have grown rather careless and certainly would if possible need some special preparation.

The last Sunday in July, on which you said in your telegram you would be free, would suit very well, if you have not since made other arrangements for that day. Hoping to hear from you soon.

I remain your Lordship's obdt servt
M.C. Kickham

The Bishop arrived on Sunday 17th June. Mr. Pope, on behalf of the Catholics of Lyttelton presented him with a handsomely illuminated address, and went on to say:

"Bishop, during many years we have looked forward to expressing a hearty welcome to the first Bishop of Christchurch. It is our first duty to thank Our Holy Father for his manifest kindness in providing for the wants of his far distant children. Our next duty is to congratulate Your Lordship on your elevation to the episcopy. We are but fulfilling the destiny of our race and becoming the means under the hands of God of bringing the faith to the uttermost ends of the Earth. Unworthy that we may be of so noble a destiny, we entertain no doubt of successfully accomplishing it while our hearts are in unison with the hearts of our Brethren at home, while we cherish the past traditions of our country, while we sympathize with her in her present struggles and foster her glorious aspirations in the future. To your Lordship do we look for the encouragement of these patriotic sentiments which unite so closely with our kindred, so that when the day will arrive and our country may be delivered from foreign administration we here may deserve to share in her triumphs and partake of the benefits which will accrue to our faith from the influence she will then exercise among the nations of the Earth."

I'm not sure the bishop was overly impressed by an appeal for *"the encouragement of these patriotic sentiments which unite so closely with our kindred"*.

Ignomy

That month I suffered the ignomy of being thrown from my horse. I was riding up Salt's Gulley and passing a fence, when the horse shied and I was thrown to the ground.[21]

All quite an embarrassment, but fortunately I escaped with nothing more than a sprained ankle. I was beginning to wonder if perhaps the problem was the rider: me! Fortunately for my confidence as well as my well-being, that was the last time a horse dislodged me!

Fundraising concert

In September, I organised a fund-raising concert for the local school in Lyttelton, which raised the princely sum of £40. It went very well, a large crowd attended and the quality of music and singing was very high indeed. The Tablet, I am happy to say, reported that it was a great success:

> Father Kickham's concert at Lyttelton was, I am glad to say, a pronounced success. The programme was a well selected one, and every item was excellently rendered. Father Kickham has good reason to be proud of the success of the concert in aid of the school funds. That success, I think, may be largely attributed to Father Kickham's personal popularity. Everyone, even those who do not belong to his church, as well as those who do, knows him for a good priest and staunch patriot and in each character he is admired and respected. He should repeat it at an early date. [22]

Application to Jesuits

With the position of seculars vis-à-vis Marist priests, and my run-in with the Bishop on St. Patrick's Day, I felt it would be impossible to continue working in Christchurch Diocese. I would have to leave New Zealand.

Having considered many different options, I made up my mind to apply to join the Jesuits. This religious order, renowned for the high learning of its members, seemed to have qualities I could aspire to and would challenge me to excel. I saw in the Jesuits an Order in which I could find the peace of mind so lacking here with the divide between secular priests and Marists. In truth, if it had not been for that discord, together with the clash with Bishop Grimes following St. Patrick's Day celebrations, it is unlikely I would have sought to leave New Zealand. Nonetheless, once the idea of joining the Jesuits formed in my mind, I believed it a noble and worthwhile venture and I resolved to succeed in it. I received a positive response to my application. [23]

Kew,
11th September 1888

My dear Fr. Kickham PC,

As Fr Jacques and Dooley's report concerning your vocation to the society is favourable I would receive you into our novitiate in Melbourne if you got leave from your Bishop and were free from the oath you took in All Hallows College to go on the foreign missions.

I do not know for how long that oath obliges you and from whom you should get the dispensation of it. Hence I think that you should write to Fr. Fortune who very likely was President of All Hallows College when you took the oath and ask of him:

1st for how many years you are obliged to work in foreign missions to justify that oath;

2nd if you kept that oath by entering the society or any other religious order on condition that you be allowed to work in foreign missions;

3rd if it be necessary to get a dispensation, how you have to set about to obtain it.

Of course if you took the oath to go and remain in foreign missions for a limited number of years, when that time is over you are free. But even in that case, I would not like to admit you into our Society without the leave of your Bishop. Please let me know at your convenience what you are going to do and what prospect of success you have. Recommending myself to your prayers and holy sacrifices.

I remain, My Dear Fr. Kickham,
Yours most sincerely in Xt ,
A Sturza SJ

I had overcome the first hurdle. Now I had to approach Bishop Grimes for his permission and I was nervous. But he was courteous, and listened closely to what I had to say.

"Father Kickham," he said, "you seem to have a genuine calling to the religious life and I will not stand in your way. However, because of our penury of priests in this diocese, I will insist that if you don't stay with the Jesuits you will return to Christchurch."

"Thank you for your support in this Your Lordship," I replied, "and yes, I do accept your condition, although I can't envisage such circumstances ever arising."

"God bless and keep me informed of your plans. I will have to arrange for another priest to take over from you at Lyttelton."

Catholic Presbytery,
Lyttelton
4th February 1889

To the Right Rev. Dr, Grimes SM

My Lord

I received your letter on Saturday morning in which you state that you have now made arrangements for replacing me at Lyttelton and ask me to fix the date of my departure. In about 5 weeks from now I shall have been two years in charge of Lyttelton and unless the arrangements you have made would be better suited by my leaving somewhat sooner, that will be the most convenient time for squaring up parochial accounts and giving them into the hands of another. As far as I am concerned, the 12th of March would be the most convenient time.

I must now express to your lordship my most sincere thanks for the consideration which you have shown me in this matter and I certainly hope that the parochial charge, which I know my inability to discharge adequately, may pass into more worthy hands.

With kindest regards

I remain your Lordship's most obdt servnt

M C Kickham

Departing Lyttelton

The word soon spread. Many reports on my departure appeared:

I have a piece of news to give to the readers of the Tablet which will cause them, I feel assured, profound regret. This regret, however, will not be unmixed with pleasure when they know the whole circumstances to which I allude. In a word then, Father Kickham is going away. He is leaving New Zealand for the purpose of joining the Jesuits. His friends will rejoice that he has received a call to join an association which comprises the ablest and best-tried men in the Church. Still, mixed with the feeling of satisfaction which must rise in the heart of a Catholic at seeing a priest advance in spirituality, there will be much natural regret on the part of Irish Catholics in New Zealand at losing a priest so well and widely loved as Father Kickham. There is in the Colony no better specimen of the thorough, frank, manly, high-spirited and high principled Irish priest than he whom we are about to lose. [24]

*   *   *

We are informed that Reverend Father Kickham of Lyttleton will shortly leave for Melbourne to join the Jesuit order there. During the past two years Father Kickham has earned the highest esteem of his parishioners in Lyttelton. [25]

*   *   *

89

On Sunday last High Mass at St Patrick's Church was celebrated by the Rev Father Kickham. This address was presented to him:

"Reverend and Dear Father, we beg to express the sincere and heartfelt regret with which we received the announcement of your departure from us. We cannot allow the occasion to pass without tendering a united expression of our love and esteem, and a high admiration for the zealous performance of the duties of your sacred office which have been exercised for our spiritual welfare, and for which no words of ours can adequately state our thankfulness. "Wishing you a prosperous career, that you may long be spared to continue the good work, and trusting you will accept the accompanying small token of our affection and gratitude." [26]

*   *   *

The expressions of regret at Father Kickham's departure are both loud and deep in Lyttelton. It is to be hoped that he will not leave us until after St. Patrick's Day, and that he will have an opportunity of making one more national speech before the very unwelcome valedictory one. [27]

St. Patricks Day 1889

There were two St. Patrick's Day celebrations that year. The celebration in Christchurch was led by Father Cummings. The celebration in Lyttelton was in Oldfellows Hall, with about ninety people at it. Best of all, there was no Bishop Grimes in control as he was away.

As Chairman, I opened the meeting proposing: [28]

"To Our Holy Father, the Pope. It is only right that we honour the successor of him who had sent St. Patrick to evangalise in Ireland."

We honoured the toast. Next I proposed:

"To Her Majesty the Queen as the representative of the Supreme Temporal Authority.

"There has been perhaps no reign that could equal that of Her Majesty in the history of the Empire. I hope that her reign will not close until the bond of union between the two sister Islands has been made a union of hearts, and that we will all live to see Home Rule."

Again, the toast was honoured. At this point I lost the run of myself. Canon Loughman, was due to propose the next toast, but before anyone could stop me I was on my feet again:

"To The Day we celebrate today

"All the blessings which flowed from Christianity and civilisation, Ireland owes to St. Patrick. But for him we might have remained in barbarism."

The toast was honoured with great cheer.

Canon Loughman just smiled. I'm sure he sensed that I was in high spirits due to my imminent departure. He responded:

"I have not had the privilege of being born in my native land, but I am no less an Irishman for that. Wherever I am, I celebrate St. Patrick's Day with the same ardour and the same faith. One St. Patrick's Day while I was in Rome, Pius IX asked me why I and my college mates were wearing shamrock. His Holiness said it was extraordinary how everywhere there were Irish. "To St. Patrick they owed everything" he said – "their faith.""

Dr. Lewis next proposed *"To Ireland a Nation*

"Ireland has been a cradle of heroes. Nearly all England's great Generals were picked from Ireland. Some of the cleverest statesmen

have been Irishmen, and the same can be said of the votaries of other
arts and sciences. I will couple this with the toast to the ladies of
Ireland, celebrated all over the world for their virtue and beauty."

Father O'Donnell, in responding said:

"Ireland a Nation means that Ireland should have the same right
that New Zealand enjoys of managing her own affairs. Ireland had her
own laws when England was in a state of barbarism. It is not
surprising that we Irish wish to have Home Rule. Since the accursed
Act of Union, England has consistently and persistently persecuted
Ireland's leaders. The leader of the whole Irish race at the present time,
Charles Stewart Parnell had to purge himself from foul assertions and
accusations made by the leading newspaper of England, backed up by
the Salisbury government. There is nothing disloyal in toasting
"Ireland a Nation". The Irish do not wish to be an independent nation,
but rather England, Ireland and Scotland should be component parts of
one great Empire."

Mr. Power proposed:

"To Parnell and his Home Rule Party
"These men have shown themselves to be men of honour, talent and
ability. After the trial, Parnell will come out grander than ever and
prove himself fit for any position. I hope we all live to see Mr. Parnell
the first Premier of the Irish Parliament."

Between the toasts Mr. Harrington, Canon Loughman and
myself sang songs with Miss O'Brien accompanying on the piano. I
couldn't contain my emotion and my longing for Ireland on this
day as I launched into a song whose words were composed by my
cousin Charles Kickham:

Alone, all alone by the wave washed shore
All alone in the crowded hall
The hall it is gay and the waves they are grand
But my heart is not there at all
It flies far away by night and by day
To the times and the joys that are gone
And I never will forget the sweet maid that I met
In that valley near Slievenamon

Everyone cheered, and some who knew the words joined in.
We continued our celebrations late into the evening.

Farewell

On the following Thursday night the Catholics of Lyttelton bade
me farewell.[29]

Mr. Burns spoke:

*"We, the Catholics of Lyttelton assemble to give expression to those
sentiments of veneration, love, and gratitude towards you, which
quicken our very pulse beat at this our final leave-taking. During the
two years of your pastorate here we hope we have learned to appreciate
your tender solicitude for our spiritual welfare, your zeal and ability in
the cause of religion, and your fostering and vigilant care over our
Catholic school. We could always reckon on your sympathy and
counsel in the many trials of everyday life. As a sterling Irishman and
patriot priest, your able advocacy of Home Rule and other kindred
subjects affecting our native land, have been warmly received and
highly appreciated by your countrymen in this colony.*

*"We warmly congratulate you on your reception into that most
illustrious Order, The Society of Jesus, whose members have been
distinguished in the world of science, literature, and art, as they have
been successful in the conversion and civilisation of the savage.
Praying that God may bestow his choicest blessing on our soggarth
aroon, and begging your blessing for ourselves and families."*

The address was beautifully illuminated by the Sisters of the Mission. It was agreed to send it home to my family and friends in Mullinahone since in joining the Jesuits I could take no "scrap" of any kind with me. Then they presented me with a purse of fifty sovereigns. This I also sent home. I responded:

"I urge you each and every one of you to remain faithful to your religious duties, and after you have discharged your duty to God, never forget what you owe to your country. Obedience to the Church and devotion to Ireland are the qualities which best become an Irishman. It is with great sadness that I now bid you farewell to continue on my religious journey with the Jesuits."

I made a small presentation to Miss O'Brien of a handsome silver card dish saying:

"Miss O'Brien, you are a good preceptor as well as precentor, and I sincerely hope that you will live a long life to carry out in the same faithful manner the duties you have heretofore so ably performed."[30]

The children attending the school presented me with a gold pencil case suitably engraved. I replied:

"I am overpowered by your expressions of goodwill. When we next meet you will be men and women."

My departure seemed to go on forever. I wanted to say good-bye to my many friends around the country.

I went to Dunedin to say good-bye to Father John O'Donnell (of Dunedin diocese, not to be confused with Fr. James O'Donnell of Christchurch) and Father Lynch. I preached in St. Joseph's Cathedral on the Sunday evening giving a sermon on the Annunciation. While there I took the opportunity to visit Kurie

Bush to say goodbye to Aunt Anne. It wasn't very far, but the poor road made it quite a journey, and I had to borrow a horse.

A few days later I was in Sumner, not far from Lyttelton, where I and many friends, including Fr. James O'Donnell and a great friend, Mr. Reynolds, dined at Mr. Heywood's house.

> *On Thursday Father Kickham passed through Christchurch. After visiting the Hot Lakes, he will take his final farewell of New Zealand. On Thursday evening he dined with Mr. Reynolds, at Sumner. Those who dined with him declare that they seldom gave a "send off" to anyone with deeper feelings of regret than to Father Kickham. It will be long before we shall look on his like again.* [31]

The send-offs were all so warm and heart-felt, that there was no small sadness in leaving such great people. I had made many friends from whom I was now departing forever

Reflecting back on my two years in Lyttelton, the contrast with Napier was quite remarkable. Yes it's true that in Napier it became quite clear to me that not being a Marist would inevitably constrain my career, however life there was free from rancour.

How different Lyttelton turned out to be. I started out with the euphoria of having control of my own parish. That soon dissipated when I became aware of the geographical extent and the low population. Income was meagre, and much of it went on travel, accommodation and food for myself and the horse. Food and accommodation were often wretched.

On top of that came the reminders from Marist priests that we were only there to assist: we were only second class priests. Did the directors in All Hallows know about this divide between Marists and Seculars when they sent us here? If they did, they said nothing to us, nor did they appear to be doing anything about it.

I knew I could not continue a life where I was considered less than an equal priest by the Marists, only there to assist. The clash with Bishop Grimes on Patrick's Day 1888 was the final straw. How could I continue in a place where I was unable to freely express my nationalist sentiments without having to consider how the Bishop might react?

I had to leave for my own sanity and well being.

The next day, the 24th of March 1889, I waved good-bye to New Zealand for ever as I embarked for Melbourne.

9 – Jesuit Novice

On the 7th of May 1889, some four weeks after my arrival in Melbourne, I entered the novitiate at St Francis Xavier College in Kew. I had spent the intervening weeks with some clerical friends, renewing acquaintances and helping them out in their ministry. I was excited by what lay ahead and had great expectations for my new life with the Jesuits.

Life there, it transpired, was totally different from my life in New Zealand in ways which I should have anticipated, but in reality I had never imagined. I had considered the further study I would be required to do, knew that it would be challenging and so it was, but I relished the challenge and was sure I would thrive. However, adapting to life in the novitiate posed unexpected challenges for me.

Reflecting on some of the entries in the diary[1] kept by the Jesuits reminds me of just how institutional life there turned out to be.

Tuesday May 7: Fr. Kickham enters on first probation. Br. Connell appointed Angel Guardian. Rest as usual.

Sunday May 12: Feast of the Patronage of St. Joseph. Holy Communion. Talk at breakfast. Recreation after dinner till 5.30. Fr. Kickham took recreation.

Friday May 17: Usual Holy Communion. Br. Connell went for a walk with Fr. Kickham because they didn't go yesterday. Benediction.

Wednesday May 22: Holy Communion offered for Fr. Kickham who put on the habit of the Society. Normal recreation after breakfast. Villa day. Benediction.

Sunday May 26: Usual Holy Communion day. Fr. Kickham went to teach Catechism.

Monday June 24: St. John the Baptist. Talk at breakfast and dinner but no extra recreation. Fr. Kickham and Brs. Baker and Petty went to Melbourne on business.

Tuesday July 2: Feast of the visitation of the Bd Virgin. Holy communion. On account of the rain, the novitiate students had an hour's recreation instead of a walk.

Friday July 5: First Friday of the month. Br. Connell finishes his retreat & sets out for St. Aloysius College Sydney. Recreation with Br. Connell from 3 till 3.30 and said good-bye at 4 PM &. Fr. Kickham drove him to the station. Benediction.

Friday July 12: Br. Petty and Fr. Kickham went to Melbourne. Talk at dinner.

I had failed to consider the obvious, that I might be going back to an institutional lifestyle, something like Melleray or All Hallows, with all the restrictions this would entail. Walks and recreation were the extent of activity. But I was now accustomed to being out among the people in the community, riding up to two hundred miles in a week and making my own day to day decisions. The change was so dramatic, the institutional life so constraining, that I came close to a nervous breakdown.

I had no option but to approach the director of novices and explain my difficulties. He had noted my struggle.

"Father Michael" he said, "I can see that you are troubled and encountering difficulties here at the novitiate. Are you sure you made the right choice in seeking to join the Jesuits?"

"When I applied, I was sure it was the correct decision for me," I replied. "And even since coming here, I find so much to interest me. The study is challenging but fascinating. But the constrained and organised life here, so different from my independent and outdoor life in New Zealand, is affecting my health and my nervous system. It pains me to say it, but I don't know if I can continue, Father."

"I understand your difficulty," he told me. "We are not accustomed to novices having lived the kind of life you lived in New Zealand, out in the open, travelling the country on horseback and having total independence. This is quite a change for you and I can readily appreciate the difficulties it must pose. I suggest that you reflect on this, on why you chose to join the Jesuits, on your current struggle and on how you see the future. Pray for guidance. We'll meet again next week"

And that's what I did. The next week I met again with the Director of Novices and also with the Father Superior of the novitiate. There was no change in how I felt. I just couldn't see how I could continue and I explained this to the Superior, who hadn't been present at the previous discussion. He understood my reasons. It was agreed that in the circumstances the best course of action would be for me to leave the novitiate.

I left on the 29th of July, less than three months after entering. I experienced no small regret and a sense of some personal failure, however I was also certain that this was the right course for me to take.

When leaving, I did not know what would come next, but I was very much aware of my commitment to Bishop Grimes: to return to Christchurch should I not persist with the Jesuits. I had given my commitment to return without much thought, so sure was I that such an eventuality would never arise.

But it did. Returning was even less appealing than persisting with the Jesuits.

I couldn't face going back to being a second class priest. I also had no doubt that I would be constantly exposed to ridicule by some Marists as the priest who had high notions but failed.

I was not going back to New Zealand.

Michael as a young man

In Angers

On arrival in Napier

In Australia c.1893

John Kickham & Catherine Flynn

Lory

Fr. Tom

Nick and Cisy

Raymie Murphy

Kattie Murphy *neé* Kickham
with son Anthony

Raymie, Kattie, Frank & Anthony

Kattie & Raymie

Annie Kirby *neé* Flynn
with daughters

David Kirby

Michael (seated)
with Australian cousins

John Kickham, Australia

Charles Kickham with nieces
Annie and Josie Cleary

Charles Kickham (right) with
brother Tom (the Dovey)

Charles Kickham
(mortuary card)

The tenanted grave

John Feeney

Louisa Feeney
neé Moughty

Feeney store
advertisement

Quinta Luisa
Residence in Olivos

Bishop Grimes

Cardinal Moran

Fr. O' Farrell in later life
as Bishop of Bathurst, Australia

Fr. James Comerford
Charters Towers

Dispensation for Michael's ordination
17 months before 24th birthday

Heading of Petition to Pope Leo XIII
(petition was submitted in French)

Secular priests in Wellington Diocese, before creation of
Christchurch as a separate Diocese with Bishop Grimes.
Fr. Michael Kickham and Fr. James O'Donnell circled.
Fr. O'Donnell was prime mover in petition to Pope Leo XIII

Gun licence

Wedding cert for Raymie and Kattie:
celebrated in Waterford Cathedral by Michael Kickham

British Club Punta Arenas: sign-in of Michael Kickham and
Dr. F. A. Gray of Armagh by Ramsey B. Nixon

10 – *Exeat*

We received no reply to our petition to Pope Leo XIII. By the time we sent it, a new Marist Bishop, Dr. John Joseph Grimes, had already been appointed and had arrived in Cristchurch a month earlier. Rome was hardly likely to roll back on that. We did hope that anyone unhappy with conditions vis-à-vis the Marists might be allowed the freedom to move elsewhere, but that never happened, at least not under Dr. Grimes as I was to discover.

We didn't even receive the consolation of an apostolic blessing which we had hoped would at least signal that someone had read and understood our petition.

Despite our best efforts to keep the petition a secret, word of it did leak out and it became clear that the Marist bishops were not happy. However, Archbishop Redwood and Bishop Grimes reacted very differently to requests to leave New Zealand.

Father James Prendergast, my successor at Napier and one of the signatories, applied for permission to leave the diocese of Wellington some six months after we sent the petition, in October 1888. This was six months before I left to join the Jesuits.

Archbishop Redwood did indeed grant him an *exeat*. He went to Sydney, where I was to meet him again a year later.

The NZ Tablet wrote of Fr. Prendergast's departure:

> *"The atmosphere in Napier is apparently not at all congenial to curates, and though some exceptionally able men such as Fathers Cassidy and Kickham have been stationed there, they have all flitted as soon as it was possible for them to do so, carrying with them the affection and sympathy of the people".* [1]

The report struck a chord even if I hadn't 'flitted': my departure was as a result of an appointment as parish priest in Lyttelton. But yet, it wouldn't take long for a new secular curate to realise that, not being a Marist, his prospects were limited.

During Father Prendergast's send-off, Mr Hoben, a member of the community, referred to *"the meagre salary given to curates, much less than would be earned by the same men in any other profession"*. This too resonated with me.

Marists would have done well to acknowledge the divide, talk to us seculars, and change their approach. We were not ogres, we would have responded positively to any engagement, but there was no sign of this.

I knew I had made the right decision in leaving New Zealand. However, I should also acknowledge that Bishop Grimes was courteous and supportive in my endeavour to join the Jesuits. I had expected otherwise. Subsequent communications were not so cordial.

South Yarra

I went to stay with an old friend Father John Fitzgerald, who had invited me to say mass in the newly restored church when I first landed in Melbourne en route to New Zealand. Now I was helping out in the parish of South Yarra. I knew of course that I must write immediately to Bishop Grimes. My agreement to the one condition put, that in the event that I didn't persist I must return to Christchurch diocese, demanded that I let him know what had occurred. Also, it was imperative that he hear it from me before he heard it from anyone else.

I wanted to let him know that my returning to New Zealand was out of the question, and hoped he would grant me an *exeat*, which would allow me to stay in Australia. Without this permission to sever my relationship with Christchurch diocese, I could not seek a position in another diocese. Just a few days after leaving Kew, I wrote to him: [2]

St Joseph's, South Yarra
Melbourne
August 5th 1889

My Lord

You will I daresay be surprised to hear that I have had to leave the Jesuit novitiate. I was utterly unable to stand it. During the three months I was there I suffered a great deal through my nervous system being completely upset. The change was so sudden from a life of activity and of a good deal of violent experience that the reaction in entering a life entirely sedentary completely unnerved me and it became completely impossible for me to follow the different exercises.

On Monday last after making 15 of the 30 days retreat I came to the conclusion with the advice and consent of the superior that there was no hope of my being able to persevere through the novitiate.

I have been feeling by no means well, feeling very dejected and low spirited but I feel better for the past few days.

I am at present staying with a friend of mine who is in charge of South Yarra parish and intend to remain with him for a short time.

As regards the future I feel very much perplexed. The thought of having to go back to Christchurch I cannot bear to enter my mind.

After coming away with the intention of not returning any more and with the object of entering the Society of Jesus, I cannot help seeing the position I would be placed in going back among these priests and people, in fact I feel it impossible to do it.

I have therefore come to the conclusion My Lord to ask your permission to seek admission into some diocese in Australia and I trust you will see your way to comply with my request.

Hoping to receive a reply at your earliest convenience,

With kindest regards,
I remain My Lord your obedient servant
M C Kickham

I did not get the favourable reply I had hoped for. The Bishop replied, agreeing that having left the Novitiate with the advice of my director, I had nothing to be ashamed of. However, he also intimated that *"my so foolishly broadcasting the news of my departure for the Society of Jesus before leaving New Zealand"* might be why I felt it impossible to return.

Broadcasting my departure? Surely he knew that even if I had slipped away quietly, all my fellow secular priests and indeed all the Marists too, would have heard about it in no time at all?

He also reminded me of my vows and my duty to the diocese, pointing out that he could ill afford to lose a priest, and that he did not have the funds to cover the cost of a replacement. I could well understand his position on this. However, for me there could be no going back.

St Joseph's, South Yarra
Melbourne
September 3rd 1889

My Lord

I received your letter in due course. As you say I do not think I was to blame in leaving the Jesuit novitiate seeing that I acted under the guidance of my director, neither in entering there for I acted under similar guidance. At the same time though I have nothing wherewith to reproach myself in the matter, I am sure you will well understand the difficult circumstance in which I would be placed in returning again to Christchurch and how much opposed it must be to one's natural feelings. I admit of course that when compared with the principles of justice which bind me to the diocese for which I was educated that this might not perhaps weigh.

Understanding as I do the difficulties against which you have to labour in your new diocese where the resources are not very great and where a good deal of expense must be incurred to procure a substitute, I have therefore determined to pay whatever justice will demand in the way of compensation so that you may procure a priest to supply my place. Within the space of three, or at the outside four years I will guarantee to contribute the amount. Though this will probably be a great difficulty for me, particularly for the first couple of years, still I would face any difficulty now rather than return to New Zealand, so concerned am I that I would not be happy there.

I trust then my Lord that you will not deny me this position of seeking admission into some diocese in Australia, it is a permission that I would not ask did I not consider it absolutely necessary for my happiness and in that way for the success of my work as a priest.

Hoping to receive an early and favourable reply.

I remain, my Lord
  Your most obdt servt
    M C Kickham

I thought that he must now see his way to granting an *exeat*. But no. He would not accept my offer, he just wanted me to comply with the condition set, to return as I had agreed, saying that principles of justice should weigh more with me than my natural feelings. And he was insinuating I joined the Jesuits with the sole objective of finding a way to leave New Zealand, that I didn't have a genuine vocation.

While it was true that if there had been no problems between us Seculars and the Marists, and if the Bishop hadn't publicly admonished me, so very unfairly, for what I said on St Patrick's day a year earlier, most likely I would not have applied to join the Jesuits. But it is also true that once I began to consider the Jesuits, I saw a life before me that was attractive and in which I was determined to succeed.

I was conscious that Father Prendergast obtained an *exeat* from Archbishop Redwood only six months after we sent our petition to Rome and it seemed now that Bishop Grimes was taking a very different approach. He was insisting on compliance with the letter of the agreement without, it would seem, any room for discussion or compromise.

This was becoming a battle of wills. I wrote yet again, this time a stronger letter, but even still restraining myself, not wanting to put to paper words I might later regret.

St Joseph's, South Yarra
Melbourne
11th October 1889

My Lord

I received your letter by the last post. I must say that I was exceedingly disappointed by your finding such difficulty in complying with my request. From what I have said in my previous letters, you cannot fail to see that I regard it as a matter of more than ordinary importance to obtain the permission I have asked for.

Admitting that the fact of my being educated for the diocese of Wellington binds me to that diocese (from which I may remark I have never been formally separated) still that obligation cannot hold me bound to anything really detrimental to my happiness.

No bishop, I am sure, would regard the rights he acquires to the services of a priest by paying for his education, particularly when that money would be afterwards refunded, as giving that absolute dominion over him which exists when he is compelled to return to his diocese against his will and willingly I certainly can never return to New Zealand. There are many other reasons besides those which I have previously given for having come to this determination, but I am convinced My Lord that you must see from this and my previous letters that the resolution I have arrived at is no mere passing feeling or delusion of mine about my future welfare, and that you will accordingly grant my request.

By sending you the money in the manner I have already guaranteed, you will be able to provide a substitute for me who will be much more content and willing to work in the diocese and consequently more efficient than ever I would be. I say this through no mock modesty proceeding from your desire for me to return, for if I were compelled to return temporarily I would continue to make every legitimate effort to obtain the permission which I now seek from your Lordship.

With regard to the probable misapprehension of my motives in entering the Jesuits if I now persevere in my desire to leave the diocese I am not alarmed. I know pretty well the extent to which that opinion would prevail and I do not consider it worth noticing.

I must therefore again My Lord renew my request. In doing so I do not think I in any way expose myself to offend against the principles of justice by which I am bound to the diocese and my case establishes no precedent for others, its circumstances being so different from any ever likely to arise again, so that I feel justified in urging you to give a favourable reply. Hoping to hear from you at your earliest convenience.

I remain My Lord,
Your humble servant,
M C Kickham

About this time, a position did arise for me in Sandhurst diocese, but I could not accept it without an *exeat*. This was now an urgent matter for me, so I sent a telegram.

Kindly reply here immediately if exeat granted reply paid Kickham. Bishop's Palace Sandhurst 14 Nov 89

But no *exeat* arrived. Just a letter, which had been sent before my telegram, again refusing me permission to leave. I was sorely tempted to just walk away, but since I had no permission to leave

Christchurch Diocese, this would also mean abandoning the priesthood. I would be unable to get a position in any other diocese. But I was committed to the priesthood, so just walking away was not an option for me.

I wrote again, not holding back anything this time, including some home truths the Bishop might not wish to hear.

Sandhurst

November 25th 1889

My Lord,

I received your letter of 11th November this morning. I am sorry to hear of your illness and hope that ere now it has passed away.

I was astonished indeed on receipt of the cablegram from Fr Aubry and yet more on receipt of your letter to see you still defer to grant me an *exeat* and that so far you fail to see any reason justifying you in giving me permission to withdraw from the diocese. How such is the case after my previous letters I cannot understand.

If my remaining in a diocese were to cause me physical suffering through ill health, that in itself would be you must admit sufficient to obtain the permission I ask for and yet there is no physical pain I would not endure, rather than the moral suffering of having, under my present circumstances particularly, to return to Christchurch. It may surprise you my Lord that I should be in that state of mind, but that was my first impulse on leaving the novitiate, it was in fact my feeling even before I left it and has been ever since.

Though I care not for the remarks of others when my conscience tells me I did my duty both in entering and leaving the Jesuit novitiate, still considering the strained relations between the religious and secular priests in the diocese

119

which during four years I saw clearly and have more than once had reason to feel, I cannot help understanding how much exposed I should be to many means of humiliation in the event of my returning which my experience of the past tells me would be not infrequently taken advantage of.

Your position and your own disposition may not enable you to understand this, but that it is so I am as certain as that I have written these words.

This in itself I consider is sufficient reason for asking for and obtaining the permission I sought. Other reasons there are in themselves perhaps more solid but which I did not wish to make any reference to previously. The principal one is that I am not happy with the position of the secular priests in the diocese; I do not consider that the secular priests in the diocese have the same status as they have in other dioceses in Australia. During the past three months I have been able to compare the relative positions of the priests in three different dioceses of Victoria with those of Wellington and Christchurch and see what are the insignificant positions the latter hold towards the former.

I myself was told more than once by some of the Marist fathers that we secular priests were only auxiliaries to help the Marist fathers to manage the diocese. Of course it would be unnecessary for me to enter into the various grounds for dissatisfaction which the secular priests in Wellington and Christchurch have, all of which were set forth in a petition sent to Rome some time ago but which did not arrive until the diocese of Christchurch had been confided to the society of Mary, so that the demands of the secular priests to be placed together in either Wellington or Christchurch and the other given to the Marist fathers, could not be granted.

I certainly would not have gone originally to the diocese of Wellington had I known exactly the position of secular priests in it and a few months ago I felt bound to advise a younger brother of mine to seek some other mission than Wellington or Christchurch.

It pains me very much to have to write on these matters, but still I feel bound under the circumstances to explain to your Lordship some of the reasons for desiring to leave the diocese.

Now particularly that I have seen other diocese and have seen how very much more satisfactory is the position of priests here, I could never feel content nor would my brother priests after I had explained matters to them, at least as far as I could help it. I do not think it fair that one body of priests should be practically governed in the interest of the other, for that is the only object in keeping Marist fathers and secular priests in both diocese.

These I think my Lord are sufficient reasons for my soliciting an *exeat* and I cannot see in the face of them how you could refuse it. Now that I am away, never can I go back to New Zealand willingly and certainly it cannot be in my interest or the interest of your diocese that I should have to return.

I trust My Lord that you will send me an immediate and favourable reply. To the conditions under which I have previously asked it, I still adhere so that there will be no injustice done to the diocese.

Hoping to hear from you soon.
I remain My Lord
Your most obdt srvnt
  M C Kickham

That did finally result in a conditional *exeat*, with commendatory letters enabling me to seek a position in another diocese. However it came with the proviso that I compensate Christchurch dioceses by paying £200,[3] a very large sum indeed, within the three or four years I had suggested. Furthermore, the conditions stated that if I did not repay amount within the agreed timeframe, I would be compelled to return to Christchurch.

I had not expected to be asked to pay so large an amount. I had volunteered to pay "whatever justice demands" and had assumed justice would require some credit for four and a half years already served in New Zealand. I also expected there would be some recognition of a priest's limited ability, or even inability, to save large sums.

Yet I had offered to pay and the price had been named. I wondered how I would ever manage to pay so large a sum, but any thoughts of going back to Christchurch were so anathema to me that I agreed. If I was unable to save £200 over the next three or four years, I would deal with that when the time came. I was just happy that for now anyway, I could remain in Sydney.

Mother and Father still knew nothing about all this. It was a year later before I wrote to them.

My Dear Parents.

I have felt so much ashamed for my extreme negligence in writing to you that I hardly know how to begin now that I have determined to write to you at last. I was so unsettled for the greater part of the past twelve months, while I was continually in hopes of settling down every day, that I have been deferring to write with the hope of having more definite information about the future to give you.

I don't distinctly remember whether I wrote to you since I left New Zealand, but I think not. At any rate I know I have not written since I left the Jesuits novitiate in Melbourne. Notwithstanding the hopes I had of becoming a Jesuit it proved absolutely impossible. After spending three months there and making every effort to persevere I saw that it was useless to struggle any longer. My health was giving way and the continued confinement and the manner of life, so different from what I had been accustomed to on the mission in New Zealand, caused me such nervous depression, that I could see that by remaining on I would probably do my health permanent injury. All the Jesuits here seemed to regret my leaving very much as I myself certainly did.

On leaving Kew I resolved that unless I were absolutely compelled, I would not return to New Zealand again, consequently I wrote to Bishop Grimes of Christchurch for permission to stay in Australia. He refused me and for about five months we exchanged letters every mail, he is trying to induce me to go back and I trying to get his permission to remain. At last I succeeded in getting a conditional permission from him with a rather stiff condition to it. It was that I should pay £200 to the diocese as soon as I was able.

Of course I accepted the condition though I fear it will be many a year before I can comply with it. If I had received the permission in time I would probably have stayed in the Sandhurst diocese, as there was an opening there at the time, but I am not sorry, as on the whole I prefer Sydney, though the priests here are by no means well off, getting only barely what supports them.

At present I am living with the auxiliary bishop Dr. Higgins, as a curate. The work is very hard as we have the largest and poorest parish in the city and the situation is by no means healthy. I do not feel quite as strong as when in New Zealand, still I have no reason to complain.

I had a letter from Laurence Kickham since his return, I was at his place in Echica while he was home and met Michael. They seem to be doing well. Pat Egan is working near Melbourne at road-making, he does not seem inclined to settle down. I have met John Kickham who was home ten or twelve years ago often since I came to Sydney. He is pretty well-to-do and has gone to live in a rising country town about 400 miles from here where he has taken a first class hotel, and is likely to do well.

I had a letter from Aunt Annie a few weeks ago. Her affairs stand exactly as when I saw her last. She says she is pretty well.

I am very anxious to know how you all are, for though I have not written I have been thinking of home and all of you as much as ever. Write soon and give me all information about how everything & everyone of you is situated. I never forget to pray for you all and I hope you will not forget to pray for me.

Your affectionate son,
Michael C. K.

Release from Christchurch

I believe that while Bishop Grimes was in Louisiana some years before his appointment to Christchurch, he contracted Yellow Fever. His health continued to be affected by this. Indeed his last letter before granting *exeat* referred to his ill health at that time. Shortly after this, it seems his health deteriorated. He went on a trip to Europe for convalescence.[4]

He was back in Christchurch in September '91, and noted I hadn't yet paid over anything. I was putting some money aside, but as I was working in poor parishes I was unable to save much. He wrote demanding payment in full by year end, or else that I return to Christchurch. This was less than two years after granting me permission to leave, even though I had said that it would take three or four years. Did he really believe I could put such a large sum aside in less than two years? Or was the £200 a trap to ensure I would have to go back? I don't know, but I simply didn't have anything near that amount saved and so I was not in a position to meet his demand. But I most certainly was not going back.

I was by now in Sydney diocese and ultimately responsible to Cardinal Moran. He was away at the time and I decided to wait for his return to discuss the matter with him.

Dr. Moran had quite an illustrious career ever before his appointment to Sydney as Cardinal. He was awarded his doctorate by acclamation, a rare honour and the mark of a truly brilliant man. He held several senior appointments including: vice-rector at the Irish College in Rome; chair of Hebrew at Propaganda Fide, also in Rome; secretary to Cardinal Cullen and professor of scripture in Clonliffe College, both in Dublin. He had advocated for a secular Bishop for Christchurch.

This was the man to whom I was now about to appeal. I knew he would only support me if he believed I had just cause, and I hoped he would see that I had. He was back in Sydney shortly afterwards and I requested a meeting with him.

"Your Eminence," I said, "when seeking an *exeat* from Christchurch, I suggested to Bishop Grimes that I would help defray the cost of my replacement. After a number of letters to and fro, he agreed to grant an *exeat* on condition that I pay the diocese £200 as compensation for the loss of a priest, a condition which I accepted. Bishop Grimes has now written to me asking me to pay up in full by the end of this year, or return to Christchurch. I am not in a position to pay and neither am I willing to return to New Zealand. Can you advise as to how I should proceed, please."

The Cardinal sat thinking for a moment before replying: "£200 is a very large sum, Michael, very unreasonable to my mind. How much do you have?"

"I have managed to save £50 over the last 2 years, that's all I have. The bishop's letter says that I had agreed to pay whatever he requested, however if my memory serves me correctly what I said was that I would pay whatever justice demanded. I also said it would take three or four years. When the Bishop wrote that compensation had been set at £200, I wondered how I would ever manage to repay such a large sum. Yet I did agree to it, I was so focused on getting an *exeat*."

"Bishop Grimes is in my view being very unfair," the Cardinal replied. "I would suggest you explain to him that £50 is all you have and ask him to accept it. I consider that should be sufficient compensation for leaving the diocese."

"Thank you very much, your Eminence."

I had hoped for support, but what he offered went far beyond my expectations. I wrote to Bishop Grimes.

St Mary's Cathedral
14th December 1891

To the Most Rev. Dr. Grimes

My Lord,

I received your letter of 15th November and would have replied by next mail but I awaited the return of his Eminence Cardinal Moran from Melbourne. I was anxious to have his advice before writing inasmuch as I had not the means of complying with your demand, viz: to provide the means for getting a substitute by the beginning of the new year.

On informing him of the nature of your letter and our previous correspondence, he said that he considered the demand you made of so large a sum of money altogether unreasonable.

After explaining to him that I had saved about £50 while I was in Sydney and that was all I possessed, he recommended me to write and ask your Lordship to accept that amount, saying that he considered it a sufficient solatium for my leaving the diocese.

Being now under Cardinal Moran's jurisdiction, I feel fully justified in following this advice that he has given me and he considers that I comply with my promise of giving a reasonable refund by giving your Lordship the sum of £50. On receipt of your reply I shall send you a bank draft for the amount.

With kind regard I remain

Your Lordship's humble and obdt srvt

M C Kickham

A few weeks later, Cardinal Moran sent word for me to come and see him. "Michael" he said, "Bishop Grimes was not at all happy with your letter, even doubting you had been accurate in quoting me. He gave me an account of all correspondence between you, it's as you had told me."

He handed the letter to me.[5]

Christchurch
29 Dec. 1891

My Lord Cardinal

One of the priests of my diocese, Rev. M C Kickham applied to us about the middle of 1889 for permission to try his vocation among the Jesuit fathers in Melbourne. Notwithstanding our penury of priests, I told him that I would not stand in the way of his greater perfection if he really felt called to being a religious, adding however that it should be with the distinct understanding that he should return to this Diocese in the event of his not persevering with the Jesuits. He seemed much pleased at the time with this.

He then went through the extraordinary course of publicising throughout all N.Z. the news of his approaching departure.

After a short stay in the Jesuit novitiate he wrote informing me that he was utterly unable to stand it. As for coming back to Christchurch he said "I feel it impossible to do it". I replied kindly assuring him that having left the Novitiate with the advice of his director, he had nothing to be ashamed of unless perhaps of his so foolishly broadcasting the news of his departure for the Society of Jesus before leaving New Zealand.

He answered that his "natural feelings" made it impossible for him to return but that he knew the difficulties and expense of procuring priests, "he would readily pay whatever I deemed necessary to procure a priest to occupy his place". Here and elsewhere I use only Fr K's own words. "Within the space of three, or at outside four years I will guarantee to contribute the amount"

Some of his fellow secular Priests said that his going to the Jesuits was a cloak for withdrawing from this Diocese. At any rate, I considered it a test case and I was of course reluctant to allow such a precedent, hence I wrote reminding F. K. that the principles of justice should weigh more with him than any mere natural feelings, and urged his return to the Diocese for which he had been educated and ordained.

He again wrote saying he could never return to Christchurch willingly. After lecturing me on my cruelty in obliging a priest to come back to a place where his lot would be "physical suffering through ill health" he explained in six pages the chief reason for his unwillingness to return was the position of the secular Priests here and in Wellington.

As your eminence is well aware I am in no way responsible for this. However acting on the advice of my Council, I consented to his leaving the diocese provided he refund a part of the expense he had put us to and the Council named £200 as the amount.

When in Rome I laid the case before the Propaganda. F. Kickham's way of acting was censured and I was instructed to order his return journey unless he fulfilled his promise when I came back to N. Zealand.

Finding that F. Kickham had sent nothing I wrote to him and received a letter of which I beg to send you a copy.

I think the good Priest must have drawn largely upon his imagination in interpreting whatever your Eminence may have replied on the question. £50 would not pay the passage to New Zealand much less for the education and outfit for a Priest for New Zealand. I shall be pleased and grateful if your Eminence will kindly advise me in this matter.

I remain, my Lord Cardinal, with deep sentiments of reverence, Your Eminence's obedient svt

+ J J Grimes, Bp. Of Christchurch

An interesting letter, I thought. He wrote that he only used my words. I never wrote that I would pay whatever he deemed necessary, rather that I would pay whatever justice demanded.

He referred to '*the position of the secular Priests*' and that '*As your eminence is well aware I am in no way responsible for this.*' Clearly he wasn't responsible as the situation existed before his arrival as

Bishop. However, I am unaware of any action he took to remedy this situation. Certainly there was no evidence of it if he did.

And he had discussed my case with the Propaganda Fide in Rome. Had he told them that I had said it would take three or four years to be able to pay? I wondered whether they also discussed our petition to the Pope, and what Propaganda Fide might have had to say about that. But if they did, the Bishop did not refer to it.

"What am I to do now, Cardinal Moran?" I asked.

"My opinion hasn't changed," he replied, before showing me the letter he had just written.[5]

St Mary's Cathedral, Sydney,

12 January '92

My dear Lord

I have this day read your lordships favour of 29th Dec & hasten in reply to state my views on this case in question.

I understand that after mature consideration your Lordship authorised Father Kickham's departure from your diocese and consequent on that authorisation he has been duly adopted in this Diocese. That there were sufficient grounds under the circumstances for his quitting the New Zealand mission appears to be unquestioned.

At our plenary council in 1885, the matter of some Bishops fixing a price to be paid by Priests when departing from their Diocese came under consideration. If I remember aright, all agreed that when a priest had served for seven years on a mission he had fully compensated the Diocese for the expense of his educational outlay. For my own opinion, I consider that when there are just reasons for a Priest to sever his connection with a Diocese, the matter of money compensation can strictly speaking have no place.

As regards Father Kickham, I am confident that he has acted conscientiously throughout and that he has no means of offering to your Lordship more than the £50 which he has said.

Allow me to take this opportunity to wish your Lordship all the compliments & blessings of the N Year.
Very faithfully yours,
+ Patrick A Cardinal Moran

This was much more than I had reason to expect or hope for. I imagine Bishop Grimes was taken somewhat aback by the Cardinal's reply, a reply he surely never expected. However he now yielded to my request and accepted my offer. I heaved a sigh of relief, and then wrote my final letter to the Bishop.

St. Mary's Cathedral
Sydney
11th February 1892

To The Right Rev. Dr. Grimes
My Lord,
I enclose a draft for £50 which you have so kindly been pleased to accept. Permit me to thank you for the kind consideration you have shown in your letter as well indeed as throughout the whole course of our correspondence on this affair of my leaving your diocese.
Kindly send the divisional letters or whatever papers may be necessary for my affiliation to this diocese to his eminence cardinal Moran, and believe me my Lord,
Your humble and obedient servant
M C Kickham

This did result in the necessary papers from Christchurch Diocese. I could now get on with my life in Sydney.

Many years later, while still in Australia, I discovered that Bishop Grimes had consulted with Archbishop Redwood before replying to my letter of 25th of November 1899 and agreeing to grant the *exeat* on condition that I pay the diocese £200. Archbishop Redwood had responded: [6]

Dec 13th 1889

My Dear Lord,

I am glad to hear that your health is better, as I was very sorry to hear of your indisposition. You must take care of yourself, not overwork yourself, and especially not fret about what cannot be changed in a day. A reasonable and moderate care and attention are far better and more efficient than excessive anxiety which often might bring on worry and its hurtful consequences of both body and soul.

I think I shall be able to get a Redemptorist Father to preach the ecclesiastical retreat in my diocese, but the matter is not quite settled. When it is, I will let you know, and then you can eask the preacher whether he can preach the retreat for your clergy likewise. I think he will.

With regard to granting an exeat to Father Kickham, this is my suggestion:

He promises to refund the money spent on his education, within a time which may be agreed upon, say three or four years; the sum has also to be fixed, about £200 I should think. Keep him to his word on this matter, but do not give him an exeat until he has paid the last instalment of the money. Tell him that he is your subject until he gets the exeat, which will be granted only when he has paid <u>all</u> the money. Meanwhile give him - if you have not done so already - commendatory letters enabling him to obtain temporary employment from another Bishop, with the promise to grant him an exeat in due form when the money has been entirely paid. Of course, also, it can be intimated to him that should he delay too long beyond the term fixed for the payment of this money, you may exercise your rights and compel either to return to your diocese or pay the money at an early date.

I would ask you to carefully preserve, <u>particularly</u>, his last letter where he gives the real motive of all his conduct, the so-called grievience against

the Marist Fathers. This document may be of great use on some future
occasion.

Hoping your health will soon be strong again, and asking a memento in
your Holy Mass.

I remain, my Dear Lord,
Yours very faithfully in JC
+ Francis Redwood
AB of Wellington

So had it been Archbishop Redwood who came up with the sum of £200? If so, Bishop Redwood was being disingenuous in saying that his Council had suggested the sum. But then, perhaps Archbishop was merely restating the sum Bishop Grimes had mentioned in a letter to him.

Either way, there was no sign of any recognition that Marist Fathers were not respecting Secular Priests. It seems expressing my feelings as a Secular priest did not go down well. Rather, both Bishop and Archbishop seemed determined to come down harshly on any expression of dissent or dissatisfaction.

For me, uppermost was my happiness that I was finally free of Christchurch and New Zealand.

11 – Australia

※※※※※※

By the time I had become totally free of Christchurch diocese, nearly three years had passed. During that time I had spent most of the first year in Melbourne, initially with the Jesuits and later working in a parish in Melbourne while waiting for my *exeat*. However, without an *exeat* I was unable to take up a position available to me there, so that by the time I received the conditional *exeat* I had moved to Sydney. I remained in Sydney diocese in various parishes for the following nine years that I spent in Australia.

Life in Sydney was very different. Whereas in New Zealand I worked in sprawling parishes with small numbers dispersed over a wide area, in Sydney parishes were compact with higher numbers. There was quite a difference between the rural parishioners, farmers and settlers, in New Zealand and the urban working class and business community parishioners of Sydney.

St. Benedict's

I worked initially as a curate with Auxilliary Bishop Dr. Higgins in St. Benedict's parish, the largest and poorest in Sydney. I was not well remunerated. The work was difficult with long hours, but satisfying in that we were ministering to a congregation who had need of much support. And of course it was a pleasure that no one was reminding me "you are only here to assist us."

I remained involved in the Hibernian Society. We had regular meetings about what was happening back in Ireland with Home Rule and the Land League, but there was less fire in the meetings here. For myself, while I still had strong views on Home Rule, I was not as inclined to make rousing speeches.

One evening, shortly after I arrived in Sydney, I attended a lecture by Cardinal Moran, about Father Damian who had worked in the leper colony on Molokai in the Hawaiian Islands. I met Father James Prendergast, who had received his *exeat* from Archbishop Redwood with an ease I could only dream of, some six months before my own departure.[1]

I thought at the time that the Archbishop was more amenable to those seeking to leave. Later, when I discovered he supported Bishop Grimes in his harsh terms for my *exeat*, my view changed. Perhaps my criticism of Marist attitudes in my letters incensed him and resulted in a hardened attitude in my case? I can't say for sure.

From New Zealand James came to Australia and was now parish priest of Araluen. This was a thriving gold mining area with up to 10,000 people, but the gold had gone and with it most of the people. A small scattered population of perhaps 1,000 remained.

We spoke about our move from New Zealand. When I explained the difficulties I had in getting an *exeat* from Bishop Grimes, he was truly shocked. Archbishop Redwood had put no such barriers in his way. Both of us were happy to be away from New Zealand and the Marists, and found Australia an altogether more pleasant environment for priests.

An Execution

In March 1891, while still at St. Benedict's, I was appointed chaplain to Darlinghurst gaol. This was a part time appointment, but it did come with an annual allowance of £50, very welcome in a poor parish. In Napier, there was an active Prison Apostolate and while there I had visited and ministered to some dozen prisoners, so I was familiar with the routine. Mostly this involved saying mass and hearing confessions as well as being a friendly face for many in a place that was far from friendly for convicts.

But there was one period at Darlinghurst that I found troubling and difficult. A seventy-two year old man, Maurice Dalton, had brutally murdered his wife, and admitted his guilt.[2]

According to reports, about 9 o'clock on the morning of the murder, Dalton and his wife quarrelled, after which the old man went out. He apparently returned an hour or two later. A Mrs. Arthur, who resided in the same house, had heard everything.

When he returned, it seems the quarrelling resumed. His wife looked for money and taunted him about being out of work. Dalton, answered: 'For God's sake let us make it up again, and live happily together', to which Mrs. Dalton apparently replied: 'I never will.' Shortly after, Dalton went out again.

Later in the day, Mrs. Arthur went into the kitchen and found Mrs. Dalton's body stretched out on the floor in a pool of blood. Her head had been battered. Nearby there was a broken plate and a frying-pan, while a bloody track across the floor led to a heavy branding iron, caked in blood, hair and brain matter.

It was a truly appalling, brutal murder. How could such an elderly man be so violent? He was found and captured without much difficulty. On conclusion of the trial, the jury found him guilty and the judge sentenced him to hang.

As Chaplain, I ministered to him in gaol. He refused to see anyone other than myself or Father Byrne, and one or other of us was always there for him.

I was with him on the eve of the execution. He seemed composed and apparently slept well enough that night. Next morning he ate a good breakfast. I found it hard to understand how he could be so calm, knowing he was about to have his life taken.

I was with him when the hangman and some warders arrived at the cell. On the way to the gallows I recited prayers out loud, and I remember his repeating them in a clear, steady voice. I stepped up onto the scaffold, just ahead of him. After the last prayer, he kissed the crucifix three times. He was calm and composed to the very end.

I stepped out of the way. The executioner then placed a white cap over his head and adjusted the noose around his neck. Dalton showed no sign of fear or nervousness. There was an eerie and unreal sense about the whole routine, as if it were a Shakespearian tragedy and the actors would at any moment face the crowd and take a bow.

But it was all too real. A moment later the hangman withdrew the bolt and Dalton dropped to his death. The corpse hung limp at the end of the rope, a truly horrific sight. The images remained with me for a long time. Sometimes I would wake up in a sweat, having had a nightmare about it all.

Knowing that he had committed such a heinous crime did not make it any easier for me to accept the execution. But I took comfort in having been there to pray with him and to support him through his final moments. Whether in his heart he repented, remains between himself and Our Lord.

Visitor from New Zealand

Some months later I had the pleasure of meeting Brother Joseph from Christchurch, who was in Australia on vacation.[3] Both of us happened to be at a concert given by the pupils of the Cathedral Girl's School. Afterwards we talked a lot about how things were back in New Zealand while I told him about my life in Sydney, how I felt life was better here for secular priests. He listened but didn't offer any opinion. Quite understandably, he wouldn't want to agree to anything critical of the Marist Order, of which he was a member. We enjoyed a day on Manly beach in weather more congenial than in Christchurch.

Tommy leaves All Hallows

I heard that my brother Tommy left All Hallows and joined the Vincentians, a religious order co-founded in Ireland by Father Roger Kickham, an uncle of Charles J Kickham. I was delighted.

[the first part of this letter has not survived]

[4] ...

You will be sorry to hear that Fr. Fitzgerald, who was home recently, has fared badly since his return. He was appointed to a curacy in Melbourne & got quite low spirited, so much so that it has ended in the complete loss of his mind. He is at present staying with a priest in Melbourne, a friend of his, but he is not expected to live very long. His uncle, Fr. Phelan does not live far from here but I have not seen him lately. He is still pretty strong. You have heard I suppose that Fr. Joe Aherne is stationed not far from me, but I have not seen him now for a couple of months, but he is getting on very well. He still sings 'The fellow that looks like me' & certainly continues to look like what the song describes in the last line.
I took a short holiday about a month ago to go to the reception of one of John Kickham's daughters in the Dominican convent at Maitland, & afterwards went to their place at Armidale nearly 400 miles from here where I spent a week. The two eldest girls who went home with them about 14 or 15 years ago are now both nuns in the same convent. The parents are doing well having perhaps the best hotel in N S Wales outside of Sydney. I was delighted to hear from Fr. Joe Ahern of all the improvements that have taken place in business for the past few years. I suppose I would hardly know the place now. The two souvenirs he brought were sadly disappointing. The pipe was broken & he evidently must have expected the reversion of the boots as they were at least two sizes too large for me.

It was rather a surprise to hear of Tommy's joining a religious order, but I daresay it is the best thing he could do. I was doubly surprised form what I had heard from his school-fellows now here of his manner and style at the choice he made.

I am glad to hear that Nicholas & Cissy are both well and happy. But now, what about Kattie, after yourselves there is no one in whose welfare I am so interested, and I am anxiously waiting to hear some news that will decide her future happiness. Of course it is great blessing for you both to have her with you, but her future must not be forgotten.

How is TPK? I trust he is keeping well. I sometimes see his name supporting the old motto 'Mullinahone never wanting in a good cause'.

Sunday next will be about the anniversary of C.J.Ks death. I will say mass for him that morning.

Remember me to all old friends at Garrymorris, Kilvemnon etc. when you see them. I hope you all continue to remember me in your prayers. I never said mass for the past nine years without remembering you all & dozens of times a year do I offer up the Holy Sacrifice for Father & Mother, brothers & sister.

Could ye not get a stray photographer to take you all in a group and send it to me. I am sending my latest 'good image'

Kindest love from your affectionate son

M. C. Kickham

Many years later, Mother showed me Tommy's letter:[5]

St. Joseph's Blackrock, Dublin
May 2nd 1892

My Dear Parents,

Well I suppose you see from the heading of this letter that I have changed my abode. I am here in Blackrock since last Friday week (22nd April), so that I am by this time a full blown Vincentian, happy and contented. The life is not a hard one, being almost the same as my college life. You need not imagine that I am doing all sorts of hard things, getting up at night and eating only half enough etc. On the contrary we have soft beds, warm clothing, and the best of food and plenty of exercise. This order lives according to that sensible principle of St. Ignatius "eat well and work well".

There are about twenty of us altogether so that we are the same family and quite at home. I trust you are not displeased with me for not telling you sooner than I did. I considered it just as well to wait and tell you all at once and put you over the thing in a hurry, because in a matter like this it is well that as few as possible should know of it.

Nobody in All Hallows knew of my going away until the night before, unless a few priests , so that when they all heard the next day there must have been a lot of talk, just like at home when a man dies or goes to cross the sea his character is discussed up and down, he is in every body's mouth for a day or so and is then forgotten.

I hope you are pleased with the change. I know you will be if you are not, because when you consider the matter seriously you cannot but see that it is a wise change and one that is caused only by God himself.

You must all pray that I may persevere and that God will give me grace and strength to end well what I have begun. And you will see that either side you or I will not regret it here or hereafter.

I remain as ever your fond son,

Tom

PS. I would say more, but I must wait until you answer this. Ask me all the questions you like and I will answer them in my next.

I was struck with how quietly Tommy had slipped away, not at all like my own departure from Christchurch. Was this how Bishop Grimes had wanted me to go? Slip away quietly, telling no one? Perhaps, but we are very different, Tommy and I.

Father Fitzgerald's poor health saddened me no end. It was he who arranged for me to say the opening mass in the newly renovated St. George's Church when I first stopped over in Melbourne en route to New Zealand. Then when I left the Jesuits, I worked with him at South Yarra while waiting to receive permission from Bishop Grimes to stay in Australia. I felt a special connection to him.

There were many many of us Irish priests in Australia. We were the backbone of the Catholic Church in Sydney. And we mostly knew one another from home, from All Hallows, or through meeting in the course of our daily lives. Some thrived but others did not fare so well. Sometimes the climate or the pressure of work would affect a priest's health. In the poorer parishes especially, the hard work and meagre income available could take their toll. As for myself, my health seemed to hold up OK, apart from the time when I had to leave the Jesuits.

A number of my Kickham cousins lived in Australia and I would meet them from time to time. John Kickham managed a hotel in Armidale, some 400 miles away. It had the reputation of being the best hotel in New South Wales, outside of Sydney.

And of course there were the many Irish who had emigrated to Australia to make a new life and better living for themselves. But still, even with so many Irish around, Australia was never home. Mullinahone was in my blood.

Liverpool

In September 1892 I became parish priest of Liverpool, some 25 miles from the Cathedral and Darlinghurst. As well as being parish priest, I was Chaplain to the Asylum for the Infirm and the

Destitute for Men and Youths. As with Chaplain to Darlinghurst, this was also a part time appointment, again with a very welcome allowance of £50 pa.

Liverpool was sometimes referred to as the Asylum Town, so dominant was the institution. It was not a prosperous place.[6]

In the asylum, men had no privacy. They slept in large dormitories. There was a farm and workshop there and those able to assist received a small recompense for their work. It was effectively self sufficient in food.

It didn't seem to matter who you were or what you had done: if you were down on your luck or simply had no one to look after you, you could end up there. There were former convicts; army officers; former politicians; lawyers; farmers; failed businessmen; and men who had come to seek their fortune in gold rushes but were left stranded and destitute. It was what stood between life and death for many, very much on the same lines as the work houses or poor houses in Ireland. It was not a pleasant place.

I visited regularly to say mass, hear confessions, talk to and comfort the residents. In such an overcrowded place, people could feel very isolated. I like to think my visits brought some small comfort to those who found little else to console them there.

Another institution in Liverpool was St. Anne's Orphanage for young girls.[6] Many of the girls came from broken homes or homes where there was alcoholism or abuse. The orphanage was run by the Sisters of Charity and catered for about 50 young girls up to the age of 15. It provided a necessary if somewhat deficient community service.

The girls were housed, clothed and educated. The nuns made it quite clear to the girls that they would have to earn their own living when they left. They received a primary education as well as being taught such skills as needlework, housekeeping and crafts. But there was never enough money to run it properly.

The Sisters were always trying to do their best with the meagre resources available, but it was difficult. There was a fundraising drive each October run by a local committee. I would attend the formal presentations, knowing however that they needed so much more than was being donated.

Camden

In 1895 I was appointed to a new position - parish priest in Camden, a town some 40 miles from the Cathedral. This was a very different place. My years working with Dr. Higgins in St. Benedict's Parish, later as chaplain to Darlinghurst Gaol and Liverpool Asylum had been tough but rewarding. These were in parts of the city where people generally were not well off, and often had just enough to get by on. Or less. I felt I was making a difference to people's lives.

Camden was a town for the relatively well off. I had my day to day responsibilities as parish priest saying mass, hearing confessions, performing baptisms, weddings and funeral services, ministering to the dying, and so on. But outside of this, life was the most comfortable I had experienced since leaving Ireland

St. Patrick's Day 1896

Cardinal Moran wanted to put on a St. Patrick's Day celebration worthy of 'Our Emerald Isle'. In 1896 he did just that.[7] For the first time, celebrations were held in Sydney cricket grounds, a large space which could cater for the crowds expected.

The Cathedral was overflowing for High Mass, and afterwards, everyone made for the cricket ground. The formal celebrations were rather sedate. I went along but with all the dignitaries present, I had no opportunity to make a speech.

The band played 'God Save the Queen' as the Cardinal received Her Majesty's Governor, Lord Hampden.[7] The Cardinal then proposed the toast to 'The Queen and the Governor.' The Governor responded:

Firstly, let me express my thanks for the manner in which the toast to me has been proposed. I admire the national sentiment of the Irishman. I felt duty bound to attend this demonstration, as I had attended the Highland Gathering; but do not think my presence here is merely out of a sense of duty. It is always a pleasure to meet Irishmen— when they are in a good humour.

But where do the English come in? Is it possible that the Englishman is content to occupy the proud position of the predominant party? Or is there something the matter with their Saint? I thought that would be a libel. Perhaps the Englishman is of too serious a character, and has no stomach for this kind of celebration.

I have heard some example of the loquacity of Irishmen in the House of Commons; but if they can talk, they can also boast of having produced some of the finest orators. If Irishmen could joke at times, they could also fight, and they had given to our common country some of our best soldiers and best commanders. As long as the English language was spoken the name of Wellington would be a household word.

The Governor seemed to be trying to be humorous, however for the vast majority of Irish present, his speech fell flat. The speeches generally were dry, delivered by people who were there only by virtue of their position and having little enough to say, or perhaps for some, uncomfortable about what they felt the crowd wanted to hear. Later, when Sir Patrick Jennings proposed the health of His Eminence, the Cardinal replied:

There are some who think it would be better to lay aside our national celebration, but I hope the time is far distant when Irishmen might forget St. Patrick's feast. It is not intended in any way to show disunion, or to prevent that 'royal blend ' which has been spoken of. I look upon the colonies as one grand Australian commonwealth with a great future. The sons of St. Patrick will be among the foremost in guarding her shores and developing her resources until she becomes the great central seat of the Empire in these southern climes. I trust the time is not very distant when United Australia will rejoice in the blessings that union will bring to her.

During the formal part of the proceedings, there was no sign of any enthusiasm for the National Cause which had been so prominent at St. Patrick's Day celebrations in New Zealand. Even the Cardinal, an ardent supporter of Home Rule, who had been consulted by Gladstone prior to introducing his doomed Home Rule bill, avoided the topic. I can only assume he did not wish to highlight an issue which the political establishment might prefer not to hear. Perhaps he was right to avoid discord on the day.

But despite this, all day long people thoroughly enjoyed themselves. There was plenty of space for large crowds to wander around and partake of the many games and fun activities happening. There was dancing, fencing, racing, jumping, tugging, and various other side shows. Friends met up and shared a picnic or a drink. These were the real St. Patrick's Day celebrations.

Philharmonic Society

I became involved in the Camden Philharmonic Society. With my interest in music I naturally gravitated towards the Society, an active and enthusiastic group. Active and enthusiastic they were but they were always looking for new members and were never able to make ends meet. Organisation was not their strength.[8]

The chairman, Mr. King, summed it up at my first AGM when he said: "Unless we get more interest in the society, it will surely collapse. And we need more members for the orchestra."

I was elected Vice-President of the society, but I must admit I was no more successful than others in developing interest in the society. Perhaps our ambitions were too much for the size of our community.

We raised funds for the Carrington Convalescent Hospital each year. One evening when we went to present the proceeds, a few of us held an impromptu concert for the patients. This was so well received that we organised a proper concert a few months later.

The society was better at collecting for others and organising events, than in actually ensuring the society itself was well organised and secure.

Sports Events

On Easter Monday 1896, together with a committee of parishioners, I organised a giant carnival to raise funds for the Church. There were many sports events and races. All went off well, with the unfortunate exception of one rider falling from his horse, fortunately uninjured. I empathised with him with my own history of horses dislodging me! The Camden News reported on the event:[9]

> "The Rev. Father Kickham was most indefatigable in his efforts to add to the comfort and enjoyment of his visitors, he was the main mover and the mainstay of the whole proceedings, in fact, he was here, there and everywhere, and the success of the sports must be undoubtedly credited to that gentleman. He was most ably supported by the judges and others."

There were Sports days at The Oaks district, which included horse and foot races and other fun events. I was heavily involved in the organisation and sponsored some of the prizes. I even won a prize for a Handicap Trot over 2 miles. Again, The Camden News reported favourably:

> "Undoubetedly the success of the day's sports is to be attributed to the energy of Father Kickham, who did everything in his power to bring affairs to a successful issue."

I took pride in the favourable reports about myself, but in truth I must acknowledge that there were many others involved in organising the events, all deserving praise.

You will understand from this account of my time in Camden how much more pleasant and relaxed an appointment it turned out to be when compared with Liverpool, or St. Benedict's, or Darlinghurst, or Lyttelton or Napier.

When in late 1898 my next appointment as parish priest in Gosford was announced, I got a great send off from the parishioners of Camden. They organised a supper at which I was presented with an illuminated address and a gift. There were about 60 people present.[10] Mr. Reidy spoke:

> "I don't need to remind any of you of the many good qualities of Father Kickham. As you all well know, we are losing a priest who has been most attentive to his high and sacred duties, and whose sterling character and kind disposition commanded respect wherever he went. For the three and a half years that Father Kickham has been with us in Camden, we have had the priceless services of a priest who devoted his great qualities to our spiritual and temporal interests."

Mr. Curran followed on, presenting me with a purse of sovereigns on behalf of the parish community:

> "Father Kickham, on behalf of all here and many who couldn't come, please accept this gift as a token of our appreciation for all

you have contributed to our community. The parishioners in Gosford will soon realise what a great priest they are getting."

I responded:

"I am honoured in the manner you have received me this evening and I thank you most sincerely for your address and presentation. It is a send off anyone might be proud of. You have always treated me with the greatest kindness and respect. Nothing could surpass the enthusiasm you displayed in support of every movement for the benefit of the Church. I feel my departure from Camden, for amongst you are to be found many of my staunchest friends. I thank especially the ladies who have so ably provided such a great feast this evening."

Father Sheridan proposed a toast to my health, which was duly honoured. We finished up singing "Auld Lang Syne".

Death of John Kickham

Just before my transfer to Gosford, my cousin John Kickham died. He had built up a reputation as a first class hotelier, starting with the Occidental Hotel in Sydney. At the time of his death he was running the Imperial Hotel in Armidale.

I had the honour of singing the Solemn Requiem Mass. [11] But as ever in such circumstances, it was the sadness of the occasion for his wife and family that dominated.

John was an ardent supporter of Home Rule and the Land League and would meet prominent members of these organisations, men such as John Redmond, Michael Davitt and John Dillon when they came to Australia.

Gosford

Gosford was another well to do parish some 80 miles from Camden, on the other side of Sydney altogether. During my few short months there I got involved in the various parish organisations and came to know many parishioners.

A longing for family and Mullinahone began to dominate my thoughts and I knew I would have to return Ireland. I had also been harbouring doubts about my priesthood for some time. These doubts were very disturbing.

I went to Cardinal Moran to inform him of my plans, however I didn't mention anything about my personal doubts and concerns. I kept these to myself. I just said I wanted to return to Ireland.

He kindly said he would be sorry to lose me, but he saw that I wasn't to be persuaded to stay. He thanked me for my many years service in Sydney Diocese, then wished me well and God speed. A few days later I received the necessary papers.

Going Home

And so it was that on the 4th May 1899 many friends gathered at the Royal Hotel in Sydney to bid me farewell.[12] Mr. Larkin occupied the chair, and the company included many of my friends and fellow priests, Father Timony, Father Bunbury, Father Carroll, Father Briody and Father Battle. Dr. Beattie from Liverpool parish was there, as were many other prominent members of the community in Sydney. I felt pride in seeing so many in attendance and it gave me the feeling that my time in Sydney had been worthwhile and that I had served my parishioners well.

Dr. Beattie presented me with a purse containing 114 guineas, and referred to what he said were the many qualities which had made my career in the colony so successful. I replied:

"I am indeed honoured and gratified in the manner you have received me this evening. I feel pride in receiving such a send off, indeed anyone would. Here amongst you are the many, many friends I have come to know in Sydney, where I have always been treated with the greatest respect and kindness.

"I thank you most sincerely for your address and presentation. You have given me a token, as you said, of the esteem in which you hold me. But I have a still more pleasant token of your esteem and regard in the kindness and sympathy expressed in your faces. I will repay you in the only way I now can, by praying for your continued health and success in life here and asking God to watch over you and keep you safe.

"Yet it is now 15 years since I last set eyes on Ireland and I am longing to be back with my family. I look forward to seeing again Slievenamon rising up behind Mullinahone and the river Anner flowing nearby. I will depart with no small regret in leaving all my friends and parishioners, but elated at the prospect of seeing Mullinahone and most of all, my family.

"Good-bye and God Bless." [13]

The next day I left Sydney on the Brisbane express. Many of my fellow priests were on the platform to see me off for the second time. I felt no small pride in being the recipient of such a warm and hearty farewell.

Charters Towers

I didn't stop in Brisbane however. Instead, I travelled a further 800 miles north to Townsville. I had arranged to stay with a friend of mine from Mullinahone, Father James Comerford, who was parish priest in Charters Towers, a mining area about 90 miles inland.

James explained the mining history of the area. Gold had been found there sometime around 1870, but as the gold was underground, it was costly enough to dig the shafts necessary to extract it. As a result, there had been no mad gold rush like there had been in Araluen where James Prendergast was. There, gold was at the surface and everyone rushed in the hopes of getting some of it. The population exploded when news of the gold got out. It dropped just as quickly when the gold was exhausted. Here in Charters Towers, gold had to be mined from underground, requiring a big company with the resources.

I had written to James, asking if I could spend some time with him before leaving Australia. He replied saying I was more than welcome, just to let him know my plans.

Of course it wasn't just to go back home that I was leaving, although that was a very important part of it. My doubts about continuing as a priest had brought me to the point where I had started to think: "I can't do this anymore". Leaving Australia would be the first step – I couldn't suddenly stop being a priest in a place where I was so well known as one.

James[13] was an old friend from Mullinahone and I wanted to spend time with him. But crucially, I felt I could discuss with him in confidence all my inner turmoil and conflicts, my doubts about my priesthood, the many things that were troubling me. And there were a lot.

The thought of just walking away from it all was comforting and gave me a feeling of relief. But it wasn't that simple. Coupled with that relief was the awareness of what leaving the priesthood would mean, not just for me but also for my family. Shame and lots of it.

Shame for the betrayal of my religion. As a priest, I was on a pedestal: a symbol and representative of the One, Holy, Catholic and Apostolic Church; authorised by the Lord himself to celebrate the Eucharist; empowered to hear confession and grant forgiveness of sins in the name of God.

What sort of person would reject this? Abandon this? Truly a shameful act, deserving of the wrath of the people. I was in turmoil, caught between wanting to act on what I believed was necessary for me to be true to myself and not wanting my family to suffer for my actions. My own shame I could deal with.

This was not something I could easily discuss with anyone. Not my parishioners certainly – they would be shocked to hear of such concerns, if indeed they had any interest in hearing them.

Nor could I discuss it with other priests. We were all friendly enough, but the kind of intimate confidence required for any discussions of concern about my vocation was distinctly lacking.

There was no possibility of having such discussions with family back in Ireland. The shame of a family member leaving the priesthood would be unbearable. Anyone else could change profession or trade, but not a priest.

I thought back on my dismissive response to mother when she wondered if I had been too young when I went to All Hallows. I had recently begun to reflect on this. Father Ignatius was right. At fifteen I really had been too young to make such a serious decision, but I'm also quite sure my decision would not have been any different a year later. It took many years for the emergence of those thoughts that I now harboured, thoughts which led to concerns about my priesthood.

All this questioning started soon after I arrived in Camden, a choice appointment after the more difficult times as Parish Priest at St. Benedict's and Liverpool. Those were poor parishes, where people were struggling, and where my income was low.

I should have been delighted with my Camden appointment, however that wasn't how I felt. Most priests would wonder if I had gone mad if I said as much to them.

It seems to me now that it was the very difficulties and challenges in New Zealand, the Jesuits, St. Benedict's and Liverpool that prevented the emergence of my questionings. I had too much else demanding my attention.

My decision to leave Australia was a first step. I had an immediate feeling of relief. However that didn't last as in reality nothing had changed. The fundamental problems remained.

I hoped talking with James would help me work through my concerns. I spent hours talking to him. He listened patiently and asked me many questions. He didn't express support, but neither did he tell me what to do. He reminded me that there was an official path to laicisation, but this was rarely granted.

Some two weeks after I arrived, I mentioned that I hadn't told them at home I was on my way. James looked at me: "Well sit down and write to them this minute," he said. I did.

Townsville N.Q.
May 18th 99

My Dear Father and Mother,

By the time this short note will reach you I will be within reasonable distance of old Ireland. I intend to leave here by the British Indian boat Duke of Buckingham on June 6th, and will get home about the beginning of August. It was only a few weeks since that I made up my mind to take the trip and make up for my negligence in not writing by having a look at you all. I am already en route and will spend the next couple of weeks before the boat leaves here, with Fr. Comerford at Charters Towers.

Meantime give all sort of best wishes to Kattie, Nicholas, wife and family and Tommy. Hoping to see you both in a fortnight or three weeks after receipt of this, in perfect health and spirits,

I remain,

Your loving though negligent son,

M.C. Kickham.

P.S. I will wire you form London or Plymouth whether I will go by Dublin or Waterford. M C K

The time came to Leave Australia, to board the Duke of Buckingham and head back home. James accompanied me back to Townsville to see me off. I thanked him for his support and patience and while he did not offer any support for leaving the priesthood, he did express empathy with my predicament and hoped I would find peace. We then embraced and said good-bye.

On board, I had six weeks to mull things over before I arrived in Plymouth. Again and again I kept going over the many issues that were troubling me. Slowly my future was coming into focus.

12 – Ireland

ack in Ireland, I headed straight for home. I couldn't wait to
see them all. Approaching Mullinahone, the views of
Slievenamon were as magnificent as I remembered. C J
Boland tells it perfectly:

"No doubt the scenes of a Swiss Canton
have a passable sort of charm
Give me a sunset on Slievenamon
from the road at Hackett's Farm"

I was overjoyed to be back. Kattie was there when I got home,
she ran to meet me and we hugged. "Michael you look great, you
must meet Raymie, we're to be married in just a few months time.
He's a magnificent man. You arrived at just the right moment, will
you celebrate the wedding for us?"

"Great to see you too Kit, but slow down a bit. Tell me who is
Raymie? And when are you getting married?"

"Raymie is from Clonmel, he calls to father in the shop from one
of the suppliers. He's really nice and polite, a true gentleman. He's
going a bit bald but that's nothing. He's been coming here for quite
some time now and just recently he asked father if he could have

my hand in marriage. When father told me I told him to say yes yes yes yes! Father and Nick thought it would be a great match. Not that it's any of their business really. I'm just so happy!"

"Kit, I'll be delighted to perform the wedding ceremony for you. When can I meet Raymie? From what you say he sounds really nice."

"Mother and Father, it's great to see you. It feels good to be back in Mullinahone," as I gave mother a hug and shook hands with father.

"Michael, it's great to see you after all this time. We haven't had a letter from you in years. We'll have to sit down and you must tell us all about it," said Mother. "Yes you certainly must," Father added.

Mother had prepared a fine Irish stew and we had apple tart afterwards. She's a great cook. We sat down to eat and we talked and talked well into the small hours of the morning.

Next morning I called over to my brother Nick and his wife, Cisy. Their family was growing, they had four children now – Kathleen, Jack, Jenny and the baby, Madeline, just a year old.

The next few weeks were hectic. I had to meet all my friends and cousins in Mullinahone and for miles around. Everyone wanted to hear all about New Zealand and Australia and I must have told the same stories hundreds of times. It was great being back, great to be among my own people. Australians and New Zealanders were really lovely people, but this was home.

I stayed in Mullinahone for a few weeks, enjoying being there, relaxing in the bosom of my family and my home town. Some time shortly after I arrived home, Raymie called to the shop. Mother invited him to eat with us, Nick and Cisy came over too.

I met Raymie, an impressive man who knew what he wanted to do. "I'm working for Boyd Ryan now, but my plan is to purchase a premises and open my own shop" he said. "There's a Mr. Grubb who has a nice place in O'Connell St. and I think he might retire soon. When he does I'll be first in to try and do a deal. He's a

Quaker and they're known for driving a hard bargain, but also for being very fair and honourable in their dealings."

Then he spoke about Kit. "I've had my eye on your sister for some time. She's a fine attractive woman. Graceful, well mannered and a strong sense of morals and religion. Your father and Nick said it would be a match made in Heaven. Kattie says you will perform the wedding ceremony and that you're talking about arranging it for the Cathedral in Waterford? That would make a fine day of it."

"I've spoken with the Cathedral administrator. He said I could arrange the wedding there. I would want nothing less for Kit."

I visited some of my old friends around the country. I called to Mount Melleray to meet Fr. Ignatius. He was delighted to see me. He had aged, but I suppose that was not surprising, it was now more than 20 years since I had been at school there.

I applied to the RIC for a shotgun licence[1] and spent many an afternoon shooting rabbits and pheasants on Slievenamon.

The wedding was magnificent, Kit so radiant and Raymie the true gentleman.[2] Tommy was stationed in the Vincentian House in Sundays Well in Cork and of course he came up to Waterford and Mullinahone for the wedding.

In the New Year I took a trip to Cork and stayed with him for a few days. We spoke about the difficulties in New Zealand and how fortunate it was that he had made the change to the Vincentians.

I got the impression that Tommy was very highly regarded in the Vincentian Order. They had been moving him around quite a bit[3] – he was in Sheffield, then Phibsboro, later Lanark in Scotland before moving to Cork in '98. Quite a lot of moving. My moving parishes every two or three years in New Zealand and Australia was much more relaxed by comparison.

However, I didn't broach my own conflicts or plans. I wasn't sure Tommy would be supportive and I did not want him trying to dissuade me. Any decision would be mine and mine alone.

To the world, I was the local boy who had travelled to the ends of the earth. I kept my problems inside and, surprisingly, managed to keep up appearances through to the wedding, Christmas and the New Year. In the spring I headed to England.

Ashton in Makerfield,
March 16th 1900

My Dear Cisy

Fancy my writing. Fr. Hanly, not Landy, is just here beside me and as he has just asked me to go over with him for a few days, I've got afraid that you might all think I was lost. I spent over a fortnight at St. Albans with Fr. Tierney and a few days between two other colonial clerical friends.

And now on my way home. I called to see Fr. O'Meara form where I write, (he is a brother-in-law to Mrs O'Meara). Fr. Hanly lives next parish and he has come over by accident to-day and now insists on my going over to him for a few days more. It turns out that he is the same John Hanly that went to school with me, in the same class for three years as Johnny Ryan of Clonagoose, so I can't refuse. How are you all getting on, send me a line to say how things are since I left. If any letters arrive for me, pack them together and send them to me first post to c/o Fr. Hanly, Ince Wigan.

Kind regards to Father and Mother, Nick and the kiddies and your mother,

Your dearly beloved brother

M.C.K

Father Hanly and I went to St. Patrick's Day celebrations in Liverpool. We decided to leave our clerical dress behind so that being less conspicuous, we could relax and enjoy ourselves. The festivities were very gay, with lots of Irish out celebrating, as well as representatives of the many companies in the area displaying their wares.

At some point during the day I felt a sudden overwhelming of my nervous system. I think it was seeing all the shipping companies and their advertisements for passages to anywhere and everywhere that got me thinking of my plans to leave the priesthood and go some place far away. I started to panic.

Father Hanly was concerned by my apparent state of mind and brought me to St. Helens Hospital, where I was seen by resident physician Dr. Francis Gray.[4] He felt I should be admitted to the hospital for a few days to rest and hopefully calm down.

Dr. Gray spent some time talking to me and helping me to get well again. He asked me many questions to try and understand what was troubling me. For the first time, I confided in a complete stranger and told him of my concerns about my priestly vocation, my plans to leave that life behind me, and that I had decided I would have to leave Ireland to avoid or at least minimise the shame on my family.

Dr. Gray, who was Irish and from the Cathedral City of Armagh, explained that as he was not a Roman Catholic, he did not fully understand why there should be so much shame. However he was aware of this phenomenon and could readily empathise with me. He said that if South America was on my mind, Liverpool was a good place to be. The Pacific Steam Navigation Company, which was based here operated regular passages to Valparaíso in Chile, calling at Lisbon, Pernambuco in North East Brazil, Rio de Janeiro, Montevideo in Uruguay, Buenos Ayres, Punta Arenas on the Straits of Magellan and finally Valparaíso. When I was better, he said, he would introduce me to a friend of his, Ramsey Nixon, who worked as an accountant with Pacific Steam.

Father Hanly called to the hospital to see me and was glad to learn that I was gradually improving. I said I would get the train to Ince Wiggan when I was discharged.

Four days later, I was back in control and was discharged from hospital. Dr. Gray, true to his word, invited me to his club to dine with himself and Ramsey that afternoon. Ramsey talked about Pacific Steam Navigation and their scheduled voyages between Liverpool and Valparaiso. He was hoping for an appointment as accountant in Punta Arenas on the Straits of Magellan. I was intrigued.

I asked about life in that part of the world and said that I was thinking of heading away from Ireland, that the thought of heading to Buenos Ayres had crossed my mind. Neither of them had been there but from everything they knew it was a magnificent city. Shipping from Liverpool to the West Coast of South America would call to Buenos Ayres or Montevideo en route.

I agreed to meet my new found friends again before I returned to Ireland. This time I revealed my concerns regarding my priesthood to Ramsey also, and how travel to Buenos Ayres was tied in with this. I felt safe enough discussing this since both were Anglicans and would be very unlikely to encounter any of my clerical friends. It transpired that we got on really well together and cemented our friendship. Over the next few years we corresponded occasionally.

I was back in Mullinahone during the summer. There were the inevitable questions about my plans for the future. When asked, I said I was waiting for some information to come through.

Southend on Sea

In September I headed to the London area. I went to see Father Patrick McKenna in Southend on Sea, whom I had met all those years ago in France. He had been studying at the Irish College in Paris while I was in Angers.

"Well Michael" he said, "you're the right man in the right place. I'm heading off to Rome for a month in October and I need someone here while I'm away. I'll tell the Bishop I know you and there'll be no problem. Would you do it?"

"Patrick, of course I'll do it." [5]

So it was that I got to spend the month of October in Southend-on-Sea. Unfortunately I wasn't going to get back for Kit's anniversary on the 26th.

> The Presbytery, Southend on Sea
> October 25th '00
>
> My Dear Kit,
> Many happy returns of the day to yourself and Raymie. I have deferred writing in hopes of having some definite information to give you – but so far nothing. I will be engaged here till Nov. 1st. During the past three weeks, I've had a very pleasant time here – just enough work, good weather and a nice country around, particularly for cycling in which I have become an adept. I hope things are all smooth at home and that Mrs. Tobin is better by this.
> Mary Russell was to have come to see me here but so far she has not been able to get away. Kind regards to Raymie, all at the hotel, Russels etc & all best wishes for many other years of married life from
> Yours
> MCK

Decisions

I was back in Mullinahone for Christmas. By now, I had finally decided that the time had come leave the priesthood.

It was the only option, but it had serious implications both for myself and for all my family. Mother and Father in particular would feel the shame, but so also would Kit, Nick, Tommy and others in the extended family. I couldn't put them through this so I couldn't remain in Ireland.

I had to decide where I would actually go. I went back over the options again for the umpteenth time. It would have to be far away. Ireland or England would be too close to home. New Zealand and Australia were out of the question, given my years there as a priest. I considered the US or Canada. However, the Irish communities there were strongly identified by their religious background. I wasn't sure they would take too kindly to one of their own who had abandoned the priesthood. Even if I tried to keep it to myself, it would surely get out.

I thought back to my meeting with Mr. Nixon and Dr. Gray in Liverpool and my discussions with them about Buenos Ayres. There was a lot of Irish emigration to Argentina, but nearly all from the midlands, not an area from where I would be likely to meet anyone I knew. There had been some priests from All Hallows who headed for Argentina, but not many and not in recent years, so it seemed unlikely I would come across any I knew.

Irish people would of course recognise the name Kicham, but they wouldn't know anything about my life as a priest. The language there was Spanish. I felt with my fluent French and the similarity of Latin languages, I would be able to learn Spanish. I had also heard that there wasn't any significant Catholic Protestant or Irish English divide there. Buenos Ayres it would be.

Crisis

Then in early 1901 my worries about leaving the priesthood and my concern for my family began to overwhelm me once again. It was much worse than I had experienced in Liverpool. How could I do it? How could I put my family in such a position? Was I being selfish in thinking only about myself?

I went through severe emotional turmoil and upheaval and was barely in control of myself.[6] Mother, Father, Nick and Kit all saw that something was very wrong and were extremely worried. Tommy was still in Cork. He had just been appointed to Lanark in Scotland but wasn't due to travel for a few weeks. He came up to Mullinahone.

They came together to discuss my condition. I was in the room with them, but barely aware of what was being said. Someone, I'm not sure who, wondered whether I should be committed to St. Lukes Mental Asylum in Clonmel. I remember vividly what happened next. Kit's voice cut through the atmosphere as she shouted out:

"MICHAEL IS NOT INSANE. WE ARE NOT GOING TO PUT HIM IN THAT APPALLING PLACE. There must be a better way to help him."

Everyone was silent, wondering what to say next. Then Tommy, who had said nothing yet, started talking:

"Michael's condition looks very serious and we shouldn't underestimate it. But I agree with Kattie, St. Lukes in Clonmel is not an option. I understand that the Monks in Melleray do occasionally allow people to stay there for an extended time under certain circumstances. I wonder whether in the current circumstances they might allow Michael to stay there, to rest up and find a route to recovery. Perhaps one of the monks might counsel and tend to him as well as be a confessor to him. I'll talk to Father Ignatius."

The others were pleased to see a solution begin to emerge and gave every encouragement to Tommy to pursue this. I was not in a position to argue, indeed I felt relief in their concern and their determination to see what could be done for me.

Father Ignatius was, I believe, very concerned to hear about my condition. He stressed that the norm was for visitors to Melleray to spend just a few days on personal retreat. However, occasionally there might be particular circumstances when someone might be permitted to stay there for an extended period. He thought that such might be allowed in my case. He brought it to the monks for consideration and there was unanimous agreement. I would be admitted for an extended stay under their care and guidance. [6]

My memories of my early stages in Melleray are vague. I was very restless, confused and disoriented. I think it took them some time to get me to settle down.

Father W was appointed my confessor and counsellor. He is a very gentle and understanding man whom I got to know very well and for whom I developed a tremendous respect. Gradually under his guidance my condition stabilised and he could begin to talk to me, listen to my concerns and start me on a road to recovery.

I do remember discussing the concerns I had about my vocation to the priesthood and my thoughts of leaving that element of my life behind me. I am also absolutely certain Father W treated everything I said as being under the seal of the confessional. There would be no information passed to anyone else either within the Monastery or outside.

For several weeks I was allowed no visitors, I had to be given time and space to come around. Father Ignatius agreed. Looking back, I can see the wisdom of this.

As my condition started to improve, I was invited to join the monks in their daily prayers and to work with them on the farm. *Laborare est orare.* The physical work was therapeutic and assisted me no end in getting back on my feet. I was surprised that I found my participation with the Monks in the routine of prayer and chant was strangely appealing and comforting. However, there was no possibility I would adapt the life of the Monks.

At this point, Father W suggested that visitors would be good for me. Kit came to visit me often as did Nick and Cisy. Tommy couldn't visit as he had moved to Lanark The journey from Mullinahone was too much for Mother and Father at their age, and they didn't visit.

Several months passed before I was able to face the world again in good health. However, I was also now confident in my decision to leave the priesthood. Fr W. was unhappy about this but understood my determination. He offered prayers and compassion and wished me well.

I returned to Mullinahone and rested for another few months before finally deciding it was time to go. Mother and Father were relieved to see how much I had improved. However, they were unaware of my decision to leave the priesthood.

In July I started to plan my departure. I wrote to Ramsey who by now was in Punta Arenas. It was September by the time I got a reply. He said it might be possible to get a reduced cost passage and gave me the name of a person to contact. This was really good news. I wrote to the contact, explaining my interest in travel to Argentina and how Ramsey had referred me to him.

I thought about what I would say to Mother and Father. I would not tell them everything, but neither would I tell them lies. In the end I said I had to go away for some time to consider my future, but that I had no definitive plans. [7] I said my good-byes to them in Mullinahone. They were happy to see me well again and hoped I would find a suitable posting.

Tommy was still in Lanark, I didn't see him again. I headed to Clonmel to stay a night with Kit and Raymie before departing. Kit was unhappy not knowing where I was going, but at the same time she was glad to see me well again. I think that at heart she knew that all my indecision since returning from Australia came down to concern about being a priest.

Next day, Nick and Cisy came in to Clonmel to say their good-byes and bid me farewell. I was heading to Dublin on the train.

On the platform Kit again asked: "How long will you be away Michael? When will you come back?"

I just gave her a hug before saying "Good-bye Kit, it may be for years and it may be forever".

"Please Michael, be sure and write, let me know how you're getting on."

"Of course I will Kit. Everything will be fine."

"I hope so. I'll pray for you every day," were her last words. With that, I boarded the train.

I can't say I was totally happy with the manner of my departure. I didn't wish to see Mother and Father or Kit or Nick or Tommy living with the shame of a family member who left the priesthood. However, although the words weren't spoken I'm sure they knew what I was intending. They would keep it to themselves to avoid the public shame. Because shame and lots of it there would be!

Sitting on the train I heaved an enormous sigh of relief, but mixed in with it was regret that I would probably never see any of my family or Mullinahone again. I was still wearing my clerical suit and Roman collar and noted the deference of other passengers towards me. I was defined by what, not who I was. This would soon change.

Thinking back now on the various stations en route to Thurles, it strikes me that the four stations were all places celebrated in C. J. Boland's recent poem, "The Two Travellers".

First stop Fethard:
The other replied: now tell me James
Were you ever at Fethard races?"

Next Farranaleen:
Said the other, "I'll lay you an even bet
You were never in Farrenaleen"

Then Laffansbridge:
Then the other impatiently said: "see here,
Were you ever at Laffan's Bridge?"

And finally Horse and Jockey:
The other replied, "Will you kindly say,
Were you ever at Horse-and-Jockey?"

This brings a smile to my face. Charles Boland was born in Clonmel and works in the civil service in Dublin.[8] I can imagine him sitting on the train, taking note of the stations and listening to other passengers rambling on about their travels far and wide, all this providing inspiration for his poem.

In Dublin I headed for the boat to Liverpool. En route, I removed my Roman collar. I was now just like any other man. The sudden disappearance of any deference towards me was breathtaking. I was down off my pedestal. In Liverpool I found a nice clean boarding house. Next day I met Ramsey's friend and booked my passage to Buenos Ayres.

13 – Buenos Ayres

I arrived in Argentina in late December. It was southern hemisphere Summer, just like Australia and New Zealand, so different from Ireland. My instincts and information proved correct. In Buenos Ayres I found that Irish people are fully respected for who they are, no sense of being second class citizens. Whether you were Irish or English, if you spoke English you were considered English. This was a little irksome, but I got used to it. [1]

A lot of Irish people lived in Buenos Ayres, and many had prospered.[1] Conradh na Gaeilge, the Gaelic League, the GAA, and Home Rule support groups were very active and the subjects of regular reports in the Southern Cross, targeting the Irish Community. I avoided involvement in favour of a life of anonymity, to limit the risk of my whereabouts becoming known in Ireland. I missed all this, and often had to restrain my natural inclinations, but it was all for the best.

Being such an enormous city, there were many neighbourhoods, some prosperous, others not so prosperous.

In some areas the Argentinean Tango, a popular and racy dance among the lower classes, was much practiced, however it was banned by the Catholic Church because of its sexual connotations, and because it was believed its origins lay in brothels and other seedy establishments. It was not to be found around Belgrano or other well-to-do areas.

As well as Irish immigrants, many, many Italians came to Argentina. They had their own particular impact on culture, food and other aspects of Argentinean society.

This was the vibrant country in which I now found myself. I settled in and started my new life. Ex-priests don't have training for too many walks of life – except teaching. I had taught in New Zealand many years previously and I would teach again.

When meeting people I introduced myself as having come from Australia. After all, I had spent ten years there. This would avoid being asked if I knew such a person in Ireland, which might lead to my whereabouts being discovered.

I found an apartment on Arcos St. in the Belgrano district and put out the word that I was available to provide private tuition in the home or at my apartment, whichever a family might choose. There was a good demand from well to do Irish families. I met many of them and became particularly friendly with the Feeneys.

James Feeney came to Argentina in '66. He went back to Ireland in 1900 to marry his cousin, Anne Moughty. They returned to Buenos Ayres and live quite near me.

The Feeneys, like many Irish here, did well. They have a large store in the city, selling quality goods of all types, and in particular Irish goods. It is one of the best purveyors of groceries in the city. They also have two large estates or *estancias*: Estancia La Dulce, near Junin on the Pampas of Buenos Ayres and Estancia Santa Elena, near Sta Eufemia in Cordoba province.

I had the good fortune to be invited to estancia La Dulce. Getting out of Buenos Ayres was a rare treat. It felt good to be in the saddle again as we rode around the estate.

The *gauchos* have a traditional beverage, *yerba mate*, an infusion which they seem to drink all the time. It's refreshing, but a little bitter. Hot water is poured over the herb in a gourd which is passed to each person in turn who drinks the contents through a silver tube. All the while conversation flows. So very sociable.

Afterwards I was treated to the delights of an Argentinean *asado*. The best of beef cooked on charcoal outdoors, washed down with Argentinean wine from Mendoza.

A Changing Society

Since I arrived in Buenos Aires so many new inventions are appearing. I remember seing a few motor cars in Sydney, none in Ireland. Here there are more and more on the streets each year. They are noisy, smelly and frightening for the horses that carry people around and draw their carriages. Is this the future? Will horses and carriages become a thing of the past? I suppose so, but I'm not sure I approve.

Then there is the electric light. Much more convenient than gas or paraffin lamps – will it soon be in every home? And the telephone – not many people have them, but those that do can talk to one another without ever having to meet.

God knows what will come next.

Punta Arenas

I corresponded with Ramsey Nixon and Francis Gray from time to time. In 1904 Ramsey applied for a position in Valparaíso and was invited to Buenos Ayres to meet some of their senior people.

He took the opportunity to meet me while here. When his appointment was confirmed, he wrote that he would be leaving Punta Arenas on board the *Oropesa* in early January,

Shortly after this, a letter from Francis confirmed he had signed up as ship's doctor with Pacific Steam. He would be on board the *Oropesa*, leaving Liverpool in November.

By a happy coincidence, both Francis and Ramsey would be on the same ship heading to Valparaiso. Francis suggested I might like to join him at Montevideo, the ship would not call to Buenos Ayres. I could travel to Valparaiso and remain on board for the return. As well as renewing friendship, it would give me an opportunity to experience new places. He hoped to be able to arrange a reduced fare or, with luck, a free passage for me. I shouldn't book in advance, just meet him when the ship docked. [2]

I wrote immediately confirming that I would take up this suggestion. I welcomed the opportunity to meet Francis and Ramsey again. And I relished the thought of discovering what would be for me, new frontiers.

The views to land as we headed south showed no sign of hills or mountains. The pampas and the Patagonian desert form one vast steppe, flat as far as the eye can see.

We passed the Valdés Peninsula, a breeding ground for whales.[3] I stood at the railings for some time watching a pair of Southern Right Whales swimming nearby and breaking surface from time to time. I was fascinated by these enormous creatures.

I learned about the large Welsh community in Patagonia in the towns of Trelew, Rawson and Gaiman near the coast and around Trevelin at the foot of the Andes. [4]

Just north of the island of Tierra del Fuego we turned west into the Straits of Magellan, a narrow channel between the mainland and the island. The water there is calmer and easier to navigate than the open seas to the south. Steam ships all take this route and stop in Punta Arenas to take on coal. There is a coal mine nearby, very strategically located for shipping.

Sailing ships mostly use the Drake Passage south of Cape Horn, despite its rough weather and unpredictable seas. They have more leeway there than in the confined waters of the Straits.

When we reached Punta Arenas, Ramsey was there to meet us. We had a brief stop-over while the *Oropesa* refuelled. We walked along the shores of the Straits, with views to Tierra del Fuego and its mountains across the water. We climbed the hill behind the town, known as Cerro Mirador, 'the hill with a view', from where the views were even more impressive.

The port of Punta Arenas was a hive of activity. It seems there has been a strong British community around that area for quite some time, attracted to the area for shipping, coal mining and sheep farming. At one time the town had been called Sandy Point, a direct translation of Punta Arenas. The streets were paved and there were electric street lights, but this had only happened shortly before Ramsey arrived. In the 1890s Punta Arenas was a frontier town, full of bars, brothels, and drunken sailors – all a far cry from when I saw it. There had even been a bar constructed of empty green bottles glued together, now long gone. [5]

I learned about the border disputes and how when everything was settled the border was agreed to be along the dividing line of the Andes. Chile had full control of the straits. I found all this fascinating.

Ramsey invited us to the British Club for lunch. This was a rather luxurious establishment, only open to members and their guests. The food and wine were excellent and we had a most enjoyable afternoon with long meandering conversations. A fitting *finale* to our brief but so impressive stop-over.

We boarded the *Oropesa* late that evening and sometime during the night the ship weighed anchor and headed for Valparaíso. The onwards voyage was a treat. Whereas the land we passed while sailing south from Buenos Ayres was flat all the way, on the Chilean side there was a myriad of fjords, islands and inlets, with glaciers and snow capped mountains in the distance. I was enthralled. What land there is between mountains and sea is so inaccessible that hardly anyone makes a living there.

Valparaíso is built on a series of hills, so different from the totally flat city that is Buenos Ayres. The city installed several funiculars to access the various hilltops. Travelling up on a few of these was a joy. From above, there were magnificent views to the city and port below and out to sea. The port was a busy place. It was a fascinating city in which to spend a few days.

Three days later the *Oropesa* was ready to depart for Liverpool, with a new complement of passengers. I said goodbye to Ramsey. It was the last time I saw him. I continued to have the company of Dr. Gray on the return journey, enjoying once more the fabulous views from the ship. In Montevideo we said our goodbyes and I returned to Buenos Ayres.

Secret revealed

I called regularly to the Feeneys. Oftentimes they invited me to stay for dinner. We had many long evenings with great discussions about anything and everything.

Anne Feeney's sister Louisa had been witness at the wedding of Anne and James in Ireland. She was just 13 at the time and remained in Ireland to continue her schooling. A few years ago, the Feeney and Moughty families arranged for John, James' younger brother, to marry Louisa. John was living in Buenos Ayres at the time and in July 1907 he travelled to Ireland to meet Louisa and escort her back to Buenos Ayres. They arrived at the end of October.

Shortly afterwards at one of my regular visits to Anne and James I met Louisa, who was living with them until the wedding. She was an attractive, well educated young woman, just 20 years old.

Louisa, it transpires, is very friendly with a Father O'Farrell back in Ireland. He is a Vincentian and knows my brother Tommy very well. She wrote to him about her new life in Buenos Ayres, and in the course of her letter she mentioned meeting me. The connection was easily made. Tommy discovered where I was and wrote a letter to be delivered to me.

One evening in February last year I was having dinner with the Feeneys when Louisa said she had received a letter from Father O'Farrell with a letter enclosed for me. She handed me a letter addressed to Father Michael Kickham c/o Miss Louisa Feeney, Buenos Ayres. I immediately recognised Tommy's handwriting. I was stunned and couldn't talk for several minutes. I didn't know what to say. The Feeneys were great friends. Omitting some details about my past was one thing but telling them lies or half truths was out of the question. [6]

Eventually I started talking and everything came gushing out. I told them about my education for the priesthood and my time as a missionary in New Zealand; about the discord between Secular priests and Marists; about the petition to Pope Leo XIII; my disagreement with Bishop Grimes and my entry to the Jesuit Novitiate in Kew.

I spoke about how I came to leave the Jesuits after just three months; my acrimonious correspondence with Bishop Grimes and my agreement to compensate Christchurch diocese; my recourse to Cardinal Moran and his support when I couldn't meet the Bishop's deadline; my 10 years in Australia; my return to Ireland; my decision to leave the priesthood; coming to Buenos Ayres. Everything. By the time I had finished, I was drained. I slumped back in the chair and waited for the response.

James, Anne and Louisa had been looking at me in disbelief as I spoke and it was now they who remained silent.

Eventually, it was Anne who spoke: "I found it difficult to believe I was listening to the same Michael Kickham I have known for the last five years. But the more I think about it, the easier it is to understand your decision to keep your past to yourself. Of course I am fully aware of the shame in Ireland attached to leaving the priesthood. But here in Buenos Ayres, while there is a strong

Catholic identity, there is also a level of tolerance which is absent in Ireland.

"For the five years we have known you, you have proven yourself to be an honourable and upright friend and a much sought after tutor for the children of Irish emigrants. It can't have been easy keeping such a secret. To disclose what you just told us, to share your past so fully, I feel emphasises the great strength of character which you have always shown."

With that she gave me a big hug, *un abrazo fuerte* as they say in Spanish. Louisa and James followed in like manner. I should note that men hugging men is part of the culture in Argentina, something that would be anathema to men in Ireland.

I asked them not to reveal my address in Buenos Ayres. I wanted to decide for myself if and when I would disclose this. Apart from this, I didn't mind what details of my life here they chose to relate, including anything I just told them. Tommy clearly already knew the significant details, so there was little point in denying him anything further.

I walked slowly back to my apartment, dwelling on what had transpired. Only when I got home did I read the letter.

The letter gave me all the news from Ireland. He wrote about how everyone was worried about me, having heard nothing for so many years, not even knowing if I was alive or dead. Father, had died three years earlier, in 1905. It saddened me that I hadn't been there, but was this just self pity? Kit had a difficult time having children. Her eldest son Frank was now five years old. However she also lost a number of babies, which must have been very traumatic. Nick and Cisy's family had grown to seven, they now had three more daughters, Eileen, Elsie and Jet.

He wrote about the anguish in the family, not knowing where I was, or even whether I was alive or dead. When I went away in 1901, they had suspected that I intended to leave the priesthood. The information from Louisa's letter to Father O'Farrell effectively confirmed that this was the case. He hadn't yet disclosed this to the other family members, he would wait for me to explain what had happened, how I had come to this. He reminded me of my priestly vows and of the family shame arising when someone leaves the priesthood. I didn't reply.

I received two more letters from Tommy since then, posted by Father O'Farrell to Louisa. In the most recent letter a few months ago, he wrote that Kit had given birth to another healthy boy last April, Anthony, a brother for Frank. I was really happy for her. If I know Kit, the two boys will be well educated, with strong Catholic beliefs and be upright members of the community in Clonmel. But will Kit tell them about her brother who departed the priesthood? Or will the shame result in me being written out of the family history?

I never replied or wrote to anyone back home. I made many attempts but I just could not do it. No doubt Louisa's letters included much information about my life here which Father O'Farrell would have passed on to Tommy. But knowing how stealthily he arranged his exit from All Hallows, I can only imagine that he was quite selective in what he disclosed.

The Wedding

Louisa and John were married last year. They invited me to join them in their celebrations, a lavish affair befitting the wedding of a wealthy couple. I found it quite a novel experience, attending a wedding and not being the celebrant. [7]

Afterwards, the reception was held at James and Anne's house, Quinta Las Rosas on Calle Arribeños. It was a very gay affair and lasted into the small hours of the morning.

John's brothers gave John and Louisa a wedding present of a fully furnished house no less. They have done well in Argentina. The house is just a fifteen or twenty minutes walk from where I live, very convenient to stroll over there of an evening.

Just recently John and Louisa bought a new house, Quinta Luisa, in Olivos to the north of the city, but they haven't moved in yet. By all accounts it is quite an exquisite property.

Re-living my departure from Ireland

Tommy's letters brought to the surface my sense of regret at having walked away from my family. Knowing that it was to protect them from the shame of my leaving the priesthood didn't make it any easier. I struggled with my own internal conflicts and suffered bouts of depression, to the extent that I ended up in hospital for a time last year.[8]

The Feeneys were my anchor, always there for me, listening to me and providing support. In recent times, I haven't always been the most cheerful person to be with. On top of all that, I recently began to worry about the state of my soul, how God would see my actions. My confession to Father Francis was timely.

I could of course have written to Ireland, or even decided to return there. But I couldn't face the thought of people looking askance at the priest who was no longer a priest, talking behind my back, and the shame that would be felt by the whole family, mother in particular. I just couldn't do it...................

What's happening?????? The light is fading......... Everything seems to be lost in a haze .... Is the nurse talking to me? I try to answer but nothing comes out...... Someone is touching my wrist.........   Now   my   eye.....   Everything   is dark...............................

14 – Death

D
r. Stuart Pennington,[1] a visiting physician at the British Hospital, looks at Michael, picks up his right arm, puts his fingers to his wrist and searches for a pulse. There is none. Michael's eyes are closed. He gently opens his right eyelid, looks in, and closes it again. He turns to the nurse and says: "Michael has gone to his reward. May he rest in peace." He records that Michael died at 2.00 am on Monday 6th December 1909.

He walks over to the window and looks out over the city of Buenos Ayres. A huge metropolis, people around at all times of the day and night. Even now in the early hours of a Monday morning, there would be Tango on the streets and the bars would be full. "The world stops for no one," he thinks to himself as he ponders the frailty of life.

His thoughts are interrupted when the nurse calls him. He has another patient to tend to.

Death Certificate

Number 2984: Kickham, Miguel Carlos.
On the 6th of December 1909, in my presence, Alfredo Deck, aged 56, married, living at Maipú 699, declared that today at 2 o'clock in the morning in the British Hospital, that Señor Miguel Carlos Kickham died of cirrhosis of the liver as certified by Doctor Stuart Pennington. I record in accordance with the law that he was male, 49 years old, a bachelor, English, educator, domiciled at Arcos 2316.

Alejandro Garañochea

Funeral

We learn with sincere regret of the death of Mr. M. C. Kickham (nephew of Mr. Charles Kickham) who passed away yesterday at the British Hospital. The deceased gentleman, who was a native of Tipperary, Ireland, came out to this country about seven years ago from Australia, and started a private school in Belgrano where he soon won the respect and esteem of the entire community. He leaves no relatives in this country, but his host of intimate friends and pupils here will deeply mourn his death. The funeral will take place today, Tuesday at 9 am from the hospital for the Chacarita. Carriages at Decks, Maipú, corner of Viamonte. [2]

Obituary

We regret having to announce the death of Mr. M. C. Kickham, relative of the novelist Charles Kickham, which sad event occurred last Monday in the British Hospital. Mr. Kickham was a native of Co. Tipperary and for some years back he had been engaged in educational work in Belgrano. During his last illness Mr. Kickham received all the consolation of the Church. The remains were laid to rest Tuesday morning in the Chacarita cemetery in the presence of numerous friends. RIP. [3]

15 – Six Months Later

S ix months after Michael Kickham's death, on the morning of Saturday 18th of June 1910, his sister Kattie Murphy neé Kickham is at home. Her husband Raymie now runs a grocery and pub at 12 O'Connell St. in Clonmel.

The family – Raymie, Kattie and their two sons Frank aged 7 and Anthony just 14 months old - live upstairs. Also living there are Raymie's brother Tim and a servant Annie Curran.[1]

It's five past nine in the morning. Raymie and Tim are down in the shop. Frank is at school. Annie is tidying up after breakfast.

Kattie is in the playroom with Anthony. She never tires of watching him wandering around, exploring everything. "He is growing up so quickly," she thinks.

She reflects back on the months before he was born, when she was so worried she might have another still born baby after the four she had already lost. Every day she prayed fervently to Saint Anthony and was overjoyed when she delivered a fine healthy son, a brother for Frank. Of course they called him Anthony.

Her thoughts drift back to Mullinahone where she was born and reared. A young salesman from Clonmel, Raymie Murphy called regularly to her father's shop. He was very attractive and he would occasionally flirt a bit with her. Then one day he asked her father for permission to marry her. She was absolutely thrilled, sure that Raymie Murphy would be a fine husband.

It was of course an arranged marriage, with a dowry being agreed by her Father, her brother Nick and Raymie. She was not consulted, however that didn't dampen her enthusiasm one whit. In any case, it was designed to encourage Raymie to set up in business.

*... **Whereas** a marriage has been arranged and is intended to be shortly had and solemnized between the said Raymond Murphy and the said Catherine Kickham*

*And **Whereas** it was agreed upon the treaty for said intended marriage that the said John Kickham and Nicholas Kickham should pay by way of fortune to the said Raymond Murphy and Catherine Kickham the sum of three hundred pounds and should covenant for the payment of the further sum of one hundred pounds to the said Raymond Murphy and Catherine Kickham in the event of the said Raymond Murphy and Catherine Kickham going into business on their own account*

*And **Whereas** upon said treaty it was further agreed that in the event of the death of the said Catherine Kickham without issue within two years from the date of the said intended marriage that then the said Raymond Murphy should pay to the next of kin of the said Catherine Kickham the sum of one hundred and fifty pounds and that in the event of the death of the said Raymond Murphy without issue but leaving the said Catherine Kickham him surviving then that the said Catherine Kickham should be entitled to receive out of the assets of the said Raymond Murphy the sum of three hundred pounds together with one half of the value of the property of every* *nature and kind of which the said Raymond Murphy is now possessed...*[2]

In August 1899, a few months before the wedding, a letter arrived from her brother Michael, saying he was on his way home. She hadn't seen him for fifteen years, since that day in 1884 when, as a recently ordained priest, he headed off as a missionary to New Zealand and later Australia.

She asked him to celebrate the wedding Mass, and of course he said yes. He organised for the wedding to be in Waterford Cathedral, no less. They were married on the 26th of October 1899. She was radiant that day, the happiest girl in the world.

In 1902 Mr Grubb announced he was selling out. Raymie approached him and they made a deal. They were now in business for themselves.

It was a fine premises, with three large display windows facing O'Connell St and separate entrances to shop and bar. There were side entrances from Flag Lane, which adjoined the premises and connected O'Connell St. to the Quay. So convenient for deliveries.

Michael had gone away by then. In 1901 he headed off but wouldn't say where he was going. He had to sort himself out, he said. "Good bye Kit. It may be for years and it may be forever," were his parting words. No one had heard from him since.

Two and a half years ago, in December 1907 her brother Tom discovered by chance that Michael was in Argentina of all places and no longer a priest! She was really concerned for his soul.

Her thoughts were interrupted by the sound of Raymie coming up the stairs. He walks in and hands her a letter. "This just arrived for you Kattie. It looks like Tom's handwriting", he says as he picks up Anthony and swings him around saying: "Who's the best boy?" Tom is Kattie's brother, a Vincentian priest.

"It's a big envelope. Tom doesn't normally write long letters", Kattie says as she opens it. "Three letters!" She starts reading.

My Dear Kattie,

I have been thinking for some time past of making known some very sad news to you, but seeing all the trouble that was round about, I thought it better to wait. Last December poor Fr. Mike took sick & was ill for around a week and died. I got a short letter from some friend of his telling of the sad fact in very few words saying merely that he got some affection of the liver. The disease was called by the doctors Hypathic Liver-wort & I suppose it means congestion of the liver. He was attended by an Irish Passionist Father, a Father Francis.

Mrs. Feeney who wrote the enclosed letter to Fr. O'Farrell was a special friend of his. It was she and her husband who first made known to Fr. O'Farrell that he was in Buenos Ayres. They seem to be very respectable people and took a great interest in him. He dined with them every week. When he went to Buenos Ayres he opened a school for sons of respectable Catholics, and I think must have been teaching them English as Spanish is principally the language of South America, and especially of the Argentine Republic.

Life and death are a great mystery and we may trust in God's mercy that he died a good death. After all his wanderings, the end came. Don't take it to heart too much. I have said many masses for him already. His death occurred at 2 am on the 6th of December 1909. May God rest him.

I haven't written to them at home yet. I suppose their letters are still held up. You might convey the news to them or if you like I will write them. Let us all say in this as in all other sad events, God's will be done. Sorrow is a part of human nature of one kind or another. Tomorrow (Saturday) morning I will be saying another mass for him & for Mother and Lory.

May God rest them all.

Yours as always

Tom

"Oh Dear God Ramie, Michael died last December!"

"Yes," he replies sombrely, "Tom told me that time he called to the shop in February".

Kattie glares at him in disbelief. "Ramie, I can't believe what I'm hearing. You've known for the past four months? And you never thought to tell me that my own brother was dead? You know how worried I've been about him. And you couldn't tell me he had died?"

She realises she is shouting now and Anthony starts crying, frightened. She lifts him into her arms and gives him a big hug. "Hush baby, it's OK".

Annie hears the crying and comes in. "Would you like me to take Anthony, Mrs. Murphy?"

"Yes please, Annie," she replies.

Raymie continues "Tom asked me not to say anything, what with all the trouble Nick was having in Mullinahone." Nick is also a brother of Kattie's.

"What have Nick's problems got to do with this? Since when does Tom decide what I should or shouldn't know? For the love of God Raymie, you are my husband. No matter what Tom said, you had an obligation to tell me."

"It wasn't just Nick's problems, your mother was very upset about everything going on at the time. Tom felt the additional shock of Michael's death would be too much for her. If I had told you, you would have felt obliged to tell her."

She sees some sense in this and her anger subsides.

Then she continues: "Tom writes *'I think he must have been teaching them English'*. It seems like he doesn't know for sure. Michael is still a mystery."

She continues to the next letter.

My Dear Kick ,

I am very sorry to hear you got a little relapse. I hope sincerely it is not serious, good men are scarce this world.

Have you heard the sad news? It is consoling to know the end was all right when it was God's will to take him away. I think you will appreciate the Feeney's action - good Irish Catholics and the proper stuff. It was well there were such cordial relations between them. The whole thing was sad but consoling at the same time.

With kindest regards and hoping you are well on the road to complete recovery,

Fr. O'Farrell.

"At least there's comfort in knowing he made his peace with God. I couldn't bear to think he might have died without that."

After a moment, Kattie continues, "Father O'Farrell's letter doesn't mention the date of death. So how did Tom know it? He must have other letters that he's not telling me about. Why doesn't he tell me everything? What is he holding back? He can be so frustrating. He was the same when he first heard Michael was in Buenos Ayres, and now about asking you not to tell me Michael had died. I can never be sure he is telling us everything."

"Tom told me he had written to Father Francis, so I'm presuming he got further information from him," Raymie replied.

"Well that's more than he's telling me, and I'm his sister. I suppose that must be it," Kattie replies. Then she looks at the letter again: "But what kind of a way is that to address anyone? My dear Kick? It must be some kind of a nickname from Kickham. Do all priests call each other by nicknames? You'd think they'd have more respect! Two holy priests. My dear Kick indeed. Don't you ever get the idea of calling me your dear Kick, Raymie."

Now there's a thought, muses Raymie to himself. Instead: "I'd never dream of it Kattie," just as she started to read the last letter.

Sta Elena, Sta Eufemia ACP,
15 March 1910

My dear Father O'Farrell,

This is the third letter I wrote you during the past six months. I addressed the others to your house in Cork and it was only a week ago Lady Molly told me you were away in Algiers. I'm making another attempt and sending this to Castlechurch marked forward.

I was so sorry to hear you were not well and that you had lost your voice. I do hope that you are now quite recovered. Please do send me a note when you get this to let me know how you are, though I don't deserve it. Still I'm not as bad as you think. I presume you never got my other letters as Lady Molly says you never get a letter from me.

I am sure you were sorry to hear of poor Annie's trouble, dear little Molly's death. She nearly broke down under it but now TG she is well again and resigned to God's will. All her other children are well and growing healthy, fine little things. We had all a hard time last winter. I nearly lost my own baby also through erysipelas[3] but TG she was spared to me. She is not a year old. Doesn't time pass quickly.

I dare say you heard of Mr Kickham's death RIP. He got ill quite suddenly and in four days was dead. It was an attack of the liver, I think. Two Dominican Fathers we sent to him and told them all about him, and then he asked to see one of the Irish Passionists. So we hope that all went right at the end. His brother's letters were delivered to him alright. Poor man we all miss him as he used to come to dinner or call in the evening to see us frequently. Well he is not forgotten and very often we get some masses said for him.

I have no news dear Father and will wind up. Joined by John, Baby Annie, and all your friends at this side of the water, kindest regards

Ever dear Father

Yours gratefully

Louisa Feeney

If writing don't write to the above address, but to Quinta Luisa, Olivos, Buenos Ayres.

Kattie is staring at the page. "This letter is from Louisa Feeney, they must have been good friends. She doesn't mention the date of death either, nor does she give the name of the Passioinst priest. There's so much that Tom isn't telling me."

"Oh Michael, I kept hoping you would come back one day and be your old self. Why didn't you stay here? At least, it's consoling to know that you made your peace with God at the end. I couldn't bear to think you might have died without the sacraments," she continues, more to herself than to Raymie.

Then she looks up: "We'll have to get a mass said for him Raymie. And you can arrange for an obituary in the Nationalist".

The Nationalist is the local newspaper and Raymie is a director. He replies: "Are you sure you want to put it in the paper Kattie? It's six months since he died. What will people think when the obituary appears so long after his death?"

A few hours later, Kattie is in the shop waiting for Frank to come home from school. He appears outside the shop chattering away with his friend Denis from a few doors up. Just then, the postman arrives with the second post with a letter for Kattie from her friend, Bridget Bowers. A friend of Bridget's, a Frather Henry, had received news of Michael's death from another priest who had been in Buenos Ayres. Kattie shows the letter to Raymie. After reading it, he thinks to himself, "just as well your letter arrived first Tom or we'd be in even worse trouble".

That night Kattie can hardly sleep thinking about Michael, praying he is now with God and the Angels in Heaven.

Next morning, Sunday, she wakes early and walks down to Abbey Street for 7 o'clock mass in the Friary. The Friary is her favourite church. Here she had prayed countless times to Saint Anthony that she would have another healthy child.[4] Now she prays to him for Michael's soul. She is sure that at heart Michael was a good man, that all will be right.

After breakfast she sits down and writes a letter to her sister-in-law Cisy, Nick's wife.

12 O'Connell St. Clonmel
19th June 1910

My Dear Cisy,

The enclosed sad news came from Tom yesterday, it is terrible to think the poor fellow was snatched away so quickly, only 4 days illness. You see by the letter he died 6th last Dec. Tom told Raymie about it when he was here last Feb. and they never told me or anybody else on account of all the trouble you had at home.

I am sorry in one way as we could have given a nice account of his death in the Nationalist at the time, which would let people know that we knew all about him. However we think it is better not to now when the thing is passed, only to get him prayed for on Sunday and tell everyone that Tom had letters and knew all about his last moments.

T.G that he had such a happy death, you will see where he asked for the Irish priest. Tom wrote to Fr. Francis for all particulars about his last moments. I can't realise that he is dead.

All my hopes are blighted now. I used to think he would come back someday and make up for his long silences. You remember what he said to me when I was seeing him off, "Goodbye Kit it may be for years and it may be forever".

A strange coincidence, Bridget Bowers, Currasilla, wrote me yesterday saying she had a letter from Fr. Henry, telling how a priest from N.Z. was on a tour and went thro' Buenos Ayres and heard of Mike's death. Fr. Tom's letter came by 1st post and hers by the 2nd. She will get him prayed for in Grangemockler.

Tom is still in St. Brendan's, Birr, Kings County. He expects to get to Clonmel for a few days after Sunday 26th.

Love to all,

Kattie

She addresses and seals the envelope, puts a stamp on it, and walks down the street to the red pillar box to post it.

She mourned Michael for a long time. The anniversaries were particularly sad occasions. In truth, although time eased the pain, she never fully came to terms with his death.

16 - Enigma

We know a lot about Michael: the great student in Melleray; the frontier missionary in New Zealand; the powerful speaker and preacher; the assiduous advocate for the National cause; the man who would not tolerate being a second class priest; who unsuccessfully tried his hand with the Jesuits, but overcame that setback; who persisted in his determination not to go back to being just an assistant in New Zealand; who was committed as a parish activist to the wellbeing of his parishioners; who cared about his siblings and helped fund their education; who was concerned for the future of his sister Kattie. For all of that he remains an enigma.

The latter part of Michael's story, from the time he left Sydney, is based on little enough concrete information.

Departure from Australia

Did Michael leave Australia just to go back to Ireland to see family, as he said in his letter of 18th May 1899? After he left Sydney it was another month before he left Townsville. Why? Just to spend time with a friend? Or had he found a particularly cheap passage home aboard the Indian ship Duke of Buckinghamshire, and was just whiling away the time until its departure? Considering that he hadn't written home before leaving Sydney diocese, coupled with his subsequently leaving the priesthood, it would seem that there was more to it.

It seems to me that he was having serious concerns or doubts about his priesthood and wanted to spend time with someone he felt he could confide in. I believe that Fr. Comerford, from Mullinahone and some years older than Michael, was that someone, hence the narrative. There is no evidence for this.

Had Michael intimated any concerns about the priesthood to Cardinal Moran? Were there reasons for his departure other than to return to Ireland, to see his family?

I have been unable to establish any archive details concerning Michael's departure. Sydney diocesan archives have very restrictive rules about access and disclosure of information. A request for information concerning Michael's departure and for a copy of his letter of excardination (a letter releasing him from Sydney diocese to enable him to take up a position in another diocese) did not yield a response.

Back in Ireland

Michael remained unattached to any diocese after his return to Ireland. He was 18 months without any visible means of support – from May 1899 when he left Sydney until October 1900 when he seemingly had a month's relief work in Southend on Sea. Was he just surviving on savings and filling in here and there from time to time?

There is the statement in that last letter to Kattie from Southend on Sea: *"I have deferred writing in hopes of having some definite information to give you – but so far nothing."*

He had used similar language when writing to his parents in September 1890, more than a year after leaving the Jesuits:

"... *every day that* **I have been deferring to write with the hope of having more definite information** *about the future to give you."*

It would seem he was expecting some information relating to his future, but I have no idea what that was. I thought perhaps he might have applied for laicisation, but could find no evidence.

Leaving Ireland

There is a letter from Michael's aunt Anne Kirby in New Zealand (from whom he got the horse, the one he had to get rid of because it kept throwing him off!), to Kattie, dated 26th January 1902. It is in response to a letter from Kattie, probably sent in October or November 1901, to reach her for Christmas. She wrote: *"Father Michael never sent me a line for the last 7 years. He must know if he asked any of the priests that know me I am glad he is out again and in good health."*

Out again and in good health suggests he was unwell and in hospital. Was he struggling with the thought of leaving the priesthood? It is not recorded.

If he was in hospital, what hospital? There was a census in April 1901, but Michael doesn't appear. But then, inststutions did not record names on the census forms, just initials. Even with this information, I was unable to find him. He could have been in England, but there is no record of him in the English census either. His brother Tom was in Scotland at the time of the census and his name is recorded. Because mental hospitals at the time were such awful places, I wondered whether he might have been given refuge in Mount Melleray. They confirmed that while the norm was for visitors to spend a few days on personal retreat, occasionally permission for an extended stay might be granted, but there would be no records. This is the basis of the storyline, which in truth lacks evidence.

The timing of Michael's departure is not recorded. The assumption in the narrative is that he didn't leave prior to the likely date of Kattie's letter to her aunt, Anne Kirby, which would explain why she wouldn't have been able to tell her Michael had gone away.

Did he tell anyone in Ireland he was leaving the priesthood? I suspect not directly, but I do think it would have somehow been apparent to his family, Kattie in particular, hence the narrative. But it is not known.

Michael's life in Buenos Ayres

We don't have much concrete information about his life in Buenos Ayres, other than that he opened a private school, was friendly with the Feeneys, and made a trip to Punta Arenas. These small snippets have allowed a plausible story to be built, based on information from today's descendents of Louisa Feeney, and other research related to his trip to Punta Arenas (see below).

Visit to Punta Arenas

He visited the British Club in Punta Arenas, signed in by a Ramsey Nixon. Signed in at the same time was Dr. F. A. Gray of Armagh. Information on Ramsey Nixon's appointment to a position in Valparaiso and his departure was reported in the contemporary newspaper in Punta Arenas, *El Comercio*.

A report in the Star of Chile, an English language newspaper in Valparaiso records the *Oropesa* voyage from Liverpool as far as Montevideo and mentions Dr. F. A. Gray, an Irishman, as being the ship's doctor. Presumably Dr. Gray and Ramsey Nixon knew each other through The Pacific Steam Navigation Company, for whom Ramsey Nixon had worked. The problem was how to fit Michael into the frame. It would seem he must have known them beforehand.

An opportunity to meet them would have occurred in March 1900 when Michael was visiting clerical friends in the vicinity of Liverpool. Ramsey Nixon was still in Liverpool. He left for Punta Arenas on the first of November 1900. Dr. Gray was resident physician in St. Helens Hospital. Information on Ramsey Nixon and Dr. Gray in 1900 was available from web searches and British Newspaper Archives.

The narrative around their meeting is fictitious, without any evidence to back it up, but it would seem plausible. If there are better explanations, I can only say I couldn't come up with one.

Secret Revealed

The timing for Michael's secret being revealed is based on the fact that Tom in his letter to Kattie (Chapter 15) wrote that it was Louisa and her husband who made known that Michael was in Buenos Ayres. Louisa arrived in Buenos Ayres in October 1907. Allowing time to settle in and meet Michael, some six weeks each way for a letter, and time for communication between Fr. O'Farrell and Tom, the assumption is that Tom discovered that Michael was in Buenos Ayres in December 1907 and that it was February 1908 by the time Michael received Tom's letter from Louisa.

I have assumed Tom wrote three letters in total. It seems likely in the timescale but I don't know this. Louisa Feeney's line in her letter: *"His brother's letters were delivered to him alright"* indicates the there were at least two. The letters have not survived, so suggestions as to what that first letter contained or the number of letters Tom actually wrote is speculative.

Whether Michael ever told the Feeneys that he had been a priest is not recorded. However Louisa's comment in her letter *"Two Dominican Fathers we sent to him and told them all about him, and then he asked to see one of the Irish Passionists. So we hope that all went right at the end."* suggests she did know.

Cirrhosis of the liver

With the cause of death being cirrhosis of the liver, the temptation is to conclude that alcohol was his downfall, and indeed that may have been so. Alcohol is implicated in about two thirds of cases of cirrhosis, but another third are due to other causes. There was quite a lot of alcoholism among Irish priests in the mining areas on the west coast of New Zealand. I asked the archivist in Christchurch whether there were any reports linking Michael (who lived on the east coast) to alcohol. There weren't.

There were a number of references to health in Michael's letters. The NZ Tablet report on Michael leaving the Jesuits says: "*The close confinement and the severe course of study proved too much for his constitution, which was never very robust…*"

The letter from Melleray to Michael's mother dated 10th March 1878 says: "*Fr. Ignatius was vexed and no wonder for he was more anxious than you were to see Michael strong and healthy and he left nothing undone to make him so.* And finishes up with: *I hope Michael's health remains good.*"

The letter from Bishop Redwood to Michael while Michael was in Angers says: "*Hoping your health is good.*" Perhaps a mere pleasantry, but nonetheless it is one of the many references to his health throughout his life.

The Southern Cross obituary of 11th December 1909 states: "*During his last illness Mr. Kickham received all the consolation of the Church*".

Referring to his last illness implies he had been ill before. Taken together all these references seem to point to health problems during his life. I considered them sufficient to avoid jumping to the conclusion that cirrhosis proves he had an alcohol problem.

Why leave the priesthood?

But behind all these suppositions lies a reason why he would want to leave the priesthood. Here there is nothing to go on. A desire to marry comes to mind, however he died a bachelor, so that seems unlikely.

Perhaps he tried unsuccessfully for a position other than just a curate in a diocese in Ireland? Was he perhaps unimpressed with the role of the priest in parishes in Ireland? That might urge him to seek a position elsewhere, but does not seem of itself a reason to leave the priesthood. Or was there something about the priesthood, about Catholicism, about religion itself which he could no longer accept?

My view is that he had his doubts (whatever they were) some years before he left Australia, possibly from around 1895, when he transferred to Camden. Perhaps the more comfortable lifestyle in this more prosperous parish allowed certain thoughts come to the fore, gave him time to think about things he was too busy to dwell on in New Zealand, or as chaplain to Darlinghurst Gaol and Liverpool Asylum.

That would coincide with the time he stopped writing to his Aunt Anne (seven years before her letter of 1902 to Kattie). The last letter we have from him from Australia was in 1892. There could have been others later which just didn't survive. However, his letter home from Townsville refers to his negligence in not writing, so I'm guessing it had been a few years at least.

I had a view that he had applied to be officially laicised or relieved of his priestly duties, and that it was information of this nature that he was awaiting when he wrote to Kattie congratulating her on the occasion of her wedding anniversary. However requests as to whether he made such applications, sent to places where such information might be, viz.: The Congregation for Clergy, Propaganda Fide and Archivio Apostolico, all in the Vatican, as well as the Apostolic Nunciature in Dublin, all drew a negative response. There may be relevant information in some archive somewhere, but where?

Michael's Story

Having digested all of the above, I developed the narrative about the latter part of Michael's life. This covers his final weeks in Australia with Father Comerford; his time in Ireland and England; leaving the priesthood; his departure for Buenos Ayres and his life there; and his visit to Punta Arenas. It is based on limited available information, but also draws on much circumstantial evidence, which is open to interpretation.

I believe the narrative to be plausible. It does not suggest any reason as to why Michael left the priesthood, which would be pure speculation, nothing to go on. Whatever the actual reason, it would seem Michael kept it to himself and there it will surely remain for all time.

17 - The Two Travellers

❦❦❦❦❦

"All over the world," the traveller said,
"In my peregrinations I've been
"And there's nothing remarkable living or dead
"But these eyes of mine have seen
"From the land of the ape and the marmoset
"To the tents of the Fellaheen"
Said the other, "I'll lay you an even bet
You were never in Farrenaleen"

"I've hunted in woods near Seringapatam,
And sailed the Polar Seas.
I've fished for a week in the Gulf of Siam,
And lunched on the Chersonese.
I've lived in the valleys of fair Kashmir,
Under Himalay's snowy ridge
Then the other impatiently said: "see here,
Were you ever at Laffan's Bridge?"

"I've lived in the land where tobacco is grown,
In the suburbs of Santiago;
And I spent two years in Sierra Leone,
And one in Del Fuego.
I walked across Panama all in a day,
Ah me! But the road was rocky."
The other replied, "Will you kindly say,
Were you ever at Horse-and-Jockey?"

"I've borne my part in a savage fray,
When I got this wound from a Lascar;
We were bound just then from Mandalay
For the Island of Madagascar,
Ah! The sun never tired of shining there,
And the trees the canaries sang in."
"What of that?" said the other, "sure I've a pair,
And there's lots of them in Drangan."

"And I've hunted the tigers in Turkestan,
In Australia the Kangaroos;
And I lived six months as a medicine man
To a tribe of the Katmandoos.
And I've stood on the scene of the Olympic Games,
Where the Grecians showed their paces."
The other replied: "Now tell me James,
Were you ever at Fethard Races?"

"Don't talk of your hunting in Yucatan,
Or your fishing off St Helena;
I'd rather see young fellows hunting the 'wran'
In the hedges of Tobberraheena.
No doubt the scenes of a Swiss Canton
Have a passable sort of charm:
Give me a sunset on Slievenamon
From the road at Hackett's Farm!

"And I'd rather be strolling along the quay,
And watching the river flow,
Than growing tea with the cute Chinee,
Or mining in Mexico.
And I wouldn't much care for Sierra Leone,
If I hadn't seen Killenaule,
And the man that was never in Mullinahone
Shouldn't say he had travelled at all!"

C. J. Boland [1]

Afterword –Writing the Book : Serendipity and Hard Graft

T he story of Michael and the mysteries surrounding his life intrigued me. In 2019 I started to take a deeper look at Michael's life and was soon hooked.

My cousin Catherine Delahanty, a grand-niece of Michael, had copies of any surviving letters home, which she shared with me.

Triona Doocey of Christchurch diocesan archives sent me a treasure trove: all Michael's letters to Bishop Grimes; a draft of Bishop Grimes' letter to Cardinal Moran (albeit incomplete and a nightmare to decipher – terrible handwriting, words crossed out etc.); Cardinal Moran's reply; a draft of the petition to Rome, and whether any of the signatories had left afterwards; Archbishop Redwood's reply to Bishop Grimes re the granting of a conditional *exeat* to Michael; and Bishop Redwood's letter to Michael while he was in Angers. I also received copies of some letters written by Father Le Menant de Chesnais.

Elizabeth Charlton of the Marist archives in Wellington provided valuable information from the time, including a photo of Michael; the list of those priests who had signed the petition and later left the archdiocese of Wellington; and more.

Peter Holm, archivist for Wellington Diocese, alerted me to the existence of the draft petition to Pope Leo XIII, which was in Christchurch. He also referred me to the Vaney doctoral thesis: *The Dual Tradition: Irish Catholics and French Priests in New Zealand : the West Coast Experience, 1865 ~ 1910. N. P. Vaney, University of Canterbury, 1976.*

A web search and information from archives turned up three theses relating to Bishop Grimes, The Marists and the Irish in New Zealand: The Vaney Thesis referenced above and the Allom and Fraser Theses, see notes 1 & 2 on Appendix I, Secular Priests and Marists.

Newspaper archives in New Zealand and Australia turned up many, many reports about Michael. These reports often recorded in great detail the words spoken at meetings and presentations. This allowed me to recreate several speeches in Michael's own words.

Michael Head SJ of the Jesuit college at Kew sent me a copy of the novitiate diary covering the period Michael was there, invaluable in understanding why Michael was *"utterly unable to stand it"*.

Dr Richard Scriven of UCC provided the necessary letter of recommendation to gain access to Vatican archives, where I found a copy of the petition to Pope Leo XIII in the *Archivo Storico de Congregatio pro Genitum Evangelizatione.* It transpired the petition had been submitted in French for some unknown reason.

Searching for the petition I came across a letter from Cardinal Moran to The Propaganda Fide in Rome. Section 4 of the letter, quoted in Appendix I - Secular Priests and Marists, gives his views on the necessity for a secular See in Christchurch.

Sydney diocese archivist Lienntje Cornelissen advised me where to find notices of Michael's various appointments and newspaper archives. There was no file on Michael in the archives. When I received the draft of Bishop Grimes letter to Cardinal Moran, Ms. Cornelissen confirmed the actual letter was in their archives, however diocesan protocols forbid copying and emailing of archived documents. I could view it but I would have to call by. Not so easy from the other side of the world. She agreed that someone could call to inspect it on my behalf and that she would waive the usual fee.

Gary Nash was in Sydney and agreed to do this. However, with his work schedule, making an appointment was not easy. I was having lunch one day with my cousin Maura Beary, who said "I know just the person to do this". A friend of hers, Keith Johnson is involved with the Australia Library of History. I wrote to him telling him about the letter from Bishop Grimes, also about Gary but that I wasn't sure whether he would be able to get to the archives. I shouldn't have doubted Gary. In the end Keith Johnson and his colleague Perry McIntyre and Gary all got there. When Ms. Cornelissen found that the last page had been misfiled she too transcribed the letter for me. So I ended up with three transcriptions.

Michael's letters from New Zealand, so well written, tell a lot about his life there and the lives of settlers, how he felt, his difficulties with the Bishop and Marists. We have nothing like this from Australia, apart from the letter about his time with the Jesuits. Nothing to indicate why he left Australia other than the few lines written from Charters Towers. I contacted Sydney archives for information on Michael's departure, but received none. Sydney diocese has very restrictive rules about access.

Michael's letter from Southend-on-Sea congratulating Kit (Kattie) on their first anniversary prompted me to contact Brentford diocesan archives. Michael's name was not recorded in Brentford archives, but it seems certain he was standing in for a priest, Father Patrick McKenna, who was on vacation in Rome for that month. Patrick McKenna had been studying in the Irish College in Paris while Michael was in Angers and both were ordained in 1884. It is highly likely that they met in France – Irish clerical students getting together.

The archivist for Southend on Sea referred me to Edward Walsh who has carried out extensive research on the Irish in Argentina. He provided much valuable information, including the existence in Mullingar Library of a complete archive of the Buenos Ayres "Southern Cross" newspaper and other sources. I later discovered a microfilm archive in Cork, much nearer home.

Letters to the Diocese of Waterford and Lismore (where Michael celebrated the marriage of Kattie and Raymie), and Cashel and Emly (Michael's home diocese), established he had never been a priest in either. Michael is recorded as celebrant for the wedding of Kattie and Raymie in Waterford Cathedral. Presumably the administrator of the Cathedral gave him permission as a visiting priest.

"The History of Mount Melleray" by Stephen J. Molony O. Cist., Paramount Printing House 1952 and a compilation of historical notes in a volume by Waterford County Council provided valuable information on life there and the strong influence Fr. Ignatius had on vocations.

Information about life in All Hallows and the Suplician Way came from "The Missionary College of All Hallows 1842-1891" by Kevin Condon c.m. (All Hallows College Dublin 1986), available on the All Hallows website. This book also lists all entrants to the College in those years, together with date of birth, where from, previous college of education, year of entry, year of ordination and where they served afterwards. This enabled me to give names of those from Melleray who entered All Hallows with Michael, and those that went to Australia and New Zealand the same year.

I could find nothing on the web about Michael's time in Buenos Aires, apart from the notices on his death and his visit to the British Club in Punta Arenas. I contacted Dominican and Passionist archives. Fr. Juan Pablo Corsiglia OP of the Dominican Provincial

Archives in Buenos Ayres suggested that Padre Sebastian Owens may have been one of the two Dominicans to visit Michael. Later, I discovered a report in the Southern Cross on the wedding of Louisa and John Feeney, which recorded that Fr. Owens and another Dominican, a Fr Murphy were present.

I wrote to two Argentine national newspapers seeking information from the public. Whether they published my letters I don't know, but I got no information.

I contacted Irish, British and American embassies. Nothing.

I searched Facebook for Feeneys in Buenos Aires, selected two at random and messaged them. One sent me information indicating she is a grand-niece of Luisa Feeney, but she knew nothing of Michael. The second wrote saying Luisa Feeney was his grandmother. However, he had no information either.

Guillermo Lynch, son of an Argentinean friend Mariano Lynch by now deceased, referred me to a Facebook group Los Irlandeses. Maria Mercedes Moughty responded to my open request, and gave me sufficient information to carry out further investigation on Irish Geneology and Irish Census websites.

Because the name Moughty is so unusual, I contacted a friend, Christie Bennett in Mullingar, who referred me to Tommy Moughty, who in turn referred me to Larry Feeney, both related to the Buenos Ayres Feeneys and Moughtys. Tommy also referred me to Donna Moughty in the US. All of them provided information about the Moughtys and Feeneys but nothing unfortunately about Michael. However the information provided context for Michael's life in Buenos Aires.

Donna Moughty provided dates for John Feeney's journey to Ireland to pick up his bride to be, Louisa Feeney and their return journey to Buenos Aires. This in turn allowed me to estimate the probable date when Michael's family learned he was in Buenos Aires – his brother Tom wrote to Kattie that it was Louisa Feeney and her husband who first made it known that Michael was in Buenos Aires.

Andrés Rodenstein of Vital Records in Buenos Ayres, procured a copy of Michael's death cert for me.

Deirdre Tallon of All Hallows Trust provided what limited information was in their archives. This included a rather curious statement that Michael had returned to New Zealand. There was no indication of where this statement emanated from. It is clear from all available information, including a response to an enquiry from Christchurch archives, that he never returned there.

Sarah Larkin of Maynooth archives (to where much of All Hallows archives have been transferred) provided a copy of the original entries concerning Michael in the All Hallows ledger. This included the note on the dispensation for ordination 17 months before his 24th birthday.

Miriam van der Molen of the Vincentian Order archives in Dublin provided details of Tom Kickham's various assignments and of Fr. O'Farrell, which showed he was from the same place as the Moughty family, Ballinacarrigy. This would explain how Louisa knew him.

I wondered whether Michael applied for laicisation and how I might discover any such application. Prof. Mary MacAleese, President *emeritus* of Ireland, also a canon lawyer, advised that relevant information if Michael had applied for laicisation, was likely to be at The Congregation for Clergy in Rome. They had nothing but in turn recommended I try Propaganda Fide and Archivio Apostolico, both also in the Vatican. Again, there was nothing. I wrote to the Apostolic Nunciature in Dublin wondering if they might have received an application from Michael, but nothing.

Michael's sign-in to the British Club in Punta Arenas was a mystery. He was signed in together with a WTA Gray from Armagh, of whom I knew nothing, by a Club member whose signature I could not decipher. I decided Gray must have been a fellow teacher in Buenos Aires who knew someone in Punta Arenas, and they both went down for a visit.

I emailed the British Club asking if they could decipher the sign-in signature. Duncan S. Campbell emailed back that it was Ramsey Boult Nixon and that one of them would have to have known Ramsey to be admitted. I searched the archives of the local Punta Arenas newspaper *El Comercio,* where I found information on Ramsey and his career and that he was heading to Valparaiso the evening of or the day following the meeting at the Club. Still no trace of any WTA Gray.

I looked for references to Grays in Valparaiso and came across quite a few, who all seemed to be jockeys. Then I saw a report in the Valparaiso *Star of Chile* by a passenger on the *Oropesa,* the ship on which Ramsey Nixon sailed to Valparaiso. The *Oropesa* was a ship of The Pacific Steam Navigation Company (PSNC), for whom Ramsey had worked when he first came to Punta Arenas. It had sailed from Liverpool and had been off the North East of Brazil for Christmas. The article was a light hearted report on the Christmas festivities on board and mentioned the ship's doctor, an Irishman, Dr. F. A. Gray.

I went back to the signature in the visitor's book, and sure enough, what I had read as WTA Gray was actually Dr. F. A. Gray. I searched the civil records for Armagh in the 1870s and found a Francis Aubodon Gray born in 1872, father a doctor. I had eventually discovered the identity of Michael's companion who signed into the British Club with him.

A ship's doctor from PSNC arrives into Punta Arenas and has lunch at the club with a former accountant of the company. No problem here, but where did Michael fit in? How did he know these people? It is inconceivable that he met them while walking down the street in Punta Arenas and that they on the spur of the moment invited him for lunch. Neither is it plausible that Michael met the doctor on the ship while he himself was taking a trip south as a tourist. The *Oropesa* did not scall to Buenos Aires on that voyage, so Michael would have had to first take a boat to Montevideo. If making his own way south he would surely have taken a ship directly from Buenos Aires – there were many direct sailings from Buenos Aires to Punta Arenas and on to Valparaíso.

There is no evidence of previous meetings between Michael and either of them, but I felt sure they must have met. A letter from Michael to his sister-in-law on the 16th of March 1900 (p. 162) puts Michael in the vicinity of Liverpool. Passenger records confirmed Ramsey didn't leave Liverpool for Punta Arenas until 1st November 1900. A search of Liverpool newspapers around that time turned up articles referring to a Dr. Gray associated with St. Helens Hospital. So now I had all three: Michael, Ramsey Nixon and Dr. Gray in the Liverpool area at the same time, March 1900. With this, I developed the story line.

Next was the question of when Michael left Ireland. A letter from Annie Kirby in New Zealand to Kattie (Kit) of January 1902 suggests she didn't know he had headed off. A line in it read *"Father Michael never sent me a line for the last 7 years. He must know if he asked any of the priests that know me I am glad he is out again and in good health."*

On first reading this I thought it could mean she believed he was back in New Zealand, wondering why he hadn't contacted her. However, Maura Beara's wiser counsel said this was much more likely to mean he had been unwell and in hospital.

Unwell: did he have a nervous breakdown due to the enormity of what he was planning? And if so, where would he have been in hospital? St. Lukes, the lunatic asylum in Clonmel? Surely his family wouldn't have that, these asylums were awful places.

Could he have been allowed to rest and recuperate in a Vincentian house (Tom was a Vincentian)? Or perhaps in Melleray? Vincentian archives had no records of anything like this ever happening. Mount Melleray have a tradition of people going there on personal retreat, but this is generally just for a few days. They did confirm that an extended stay, though rare, was possible under certain circumstances, but there would be no records.

I assumed that between Michael's cheques to support Tom's 'pension' (boarding costs) and the letter from T B Laurence to Michael's mother, the conditions existed for the Cistercians to accept Michael for an extended stay. Whether it happened like that I can't say, but it seems plausible.

Michael would then have been well enough to travel towards the end of 1901, arriving in Buenos Aires in late 1901 or early 1902. This would dovetail with the notice of Michael's funeral in the Southern Cross, 7th December 1909 which stated that he had started a private school in Belgrano seven years previously. I have been unable to find any reference to Michael's school.

And there are the many people I contacted looking for information that just wasn't there, but they took the time to search and let me know: Fr. Uinsean, Melleray archivist; Fr. Rob of the Passionist Order; Michael Knies of Scranton University; Matthew and Fr. Brian of the Passionist archives in Mount Argus; Padre Alejandro Dario of Parroquia Santa Elena in Buenos Ayres; Rachel Naughton of Melbourne Cathedral Parish Office; Colleen Kirk of Gosford parish.

Michael Nolan proof-read the document in great detail and made many valuable suggestions, not least his strong recommendation as to what the title of the book should be, which I accepted. Garret Murphy and Annemarie Barrett looked at my rather prosaic draft cover design and pointed me in a better direction.

To all who helped me along the way, I offer my sincere thanks. Without you this book could not have been written. However, any errors or shortcomings are my responsibility.

Vincent Murphy
November 2021

*If you have enjoyed the book, and I hope you have, please go to the comments page of the website **www.flaglane.ie** where you can write a review, or indeed comment otherwise.*

Appendix I - Secular Priests and Marists

It will be clear to the reader that there were tensions among the clergy in New Zealand at the time, between the Secular Priests and Marists. What follows is but a brief review of some aspects of the conflict.

The Secular Priests' petition to Rome was not the first that Propaganda Fide in Rome knew of the tensions. In 1885, the first plenary council of Australasian bishops recommended that the appointment of a new Bishop for New Zealand go to a diocesan (secular) priest. This would have strengthened the largely Irish diocesan clergy at the expense of the Marists.

On 10th March 1887, Cardinal Moran of Sydney wrote to 'His Eminence', presumably the same Cardinal Simeoni to whom the petition was addressed, at Propaganda Fide. The letter (a copy of which has been obtained from Vatican archives) covers a number of issues, item 4 is of particular interest here:

4. It is necessary to provide also for setting up the new see of Christchurch in New Zealand. The dissensions between the secular clergy and the Marist Fathers are increasing daily, and between Catholics themselves. If a zealous bishop from the secular clergy is not provided very quickly for that diocese, the religion will suffer great damage. There are reports that the Marist Fathers boast of having achieved a complete triumph in Rome in regard to the new diocese. In truth, I don't know how much there is to these boasts, however I have not had an answer from Your Eminence on this matter. But this should tell us that the nomination of a bishop to Christchurch is necessary for the good of our holy religion, and that the nomination of a Marist priest as Bishop of that See would be the cause of the most grave disorder in that diocese.

When he writes '*I have not had an answer from Your Eminence on this matter*', it is reasonable to assume he had previously raised the matter with the Propaganda. It could be said that Cardinal Moran as an Irish Secular himself was just fighting for his own side.

Perhaps. However he was surely aware of the attitude of Marists to Secular Priests, that they were there as mere assistants, and would not want to see this situation continue. Without the pastoral care of a Bishop who would value them, the alienation of Seculars would continue with adverse consequences.

Both the Plenary Council of Australasian Bishops and Cardinal Moran's letter to Propaganda Fide pre-date the appointment of Bishop Grimes, but they fell on deaf ears.

The Marists also sought influence in Rome and in the end they prevailed. On the 27th July 1887, John Joseph Grimes was duly installed as bishop of Christchurch while Bishop Redwood was elevated to Archbishop and Metropolitan of Wellington, both Marists.

In his letter home of 18th April 1888 Michael talks about ecclesiastical matters and the position of the Irish Priests and says:

"*The matter is at present before the Holy See at Rome.*"

This clearly referred to the petition to Pope Leo XIII of March 1888, signed by eighteen secular priests, Michael included. The full text can be read in Appendix II.

An issue which was not referred to in the petition to Rome, is that Marists take a vow of poverty. Secular Priests don't. Yet the Marists seem to have kept all the more prosperous parishes for themselves and left the Irish Seculars to fend as best they could in the more marginal areas. The parishes on the west coast it seems were particularly difficult, gold rush, lots of alcohol, isolation. There was significant alcohol abuse among the Irish priests. The drunken Irish? Or the consequence of social isolation and depression?

In the Allom[1] thesis, Bishop Grimes is quoted as saying about his search for priests for some of the more remote parishes:

"...Ahaura, formerly served and well served by our Fathers like Ross, now alas too badly served by Seculars both of whom I am obliged to remove, having no one to put in the place of the latter. This is one of the reasons I am eager to go to Europe to try and get a few good seculars. We want Saints and Teetotallers and especially Teetotallers"

Ahuara was in the gold mining area of the West Coast, where Father O'Donnell had served before being removed by Bishop Redwood prior to Bishop Grimes arriving in Christchurch.

It would seem that the Bishop took for granted the community support the Marists enjoyed within their order. This would help them feel more secure, while the seculars with no such attachment could all too easily feel alone and isolated. Being told they were only there to assist was hardly likely to help their self-confidence.

Did this make it more likely they would succumb to alcohol? It would depend on the individual. Some would inevitably be more resilient than others. Without support and pastoral care, and a belief in their value, it would be easy enough to fall.

And did their clerical training in Maynooth or All Hallows prepare them for such risks and how to cope? Or were they sent out to fend for themselves? Michael's two years in Angers involved training for life as a priest, which I'm sure served him well. But this aspect of the Suplician Way was not included in the All Hallows programme and therefore was not available to most Irish missionaries.

These were difficult situations. Values, practices, expectations in the late 19th century were all rather different from what we might expect today. Bishop Grimes wanting only saints and teetotalers would seem to have set the bar higher than was reasonable to expect, without support structures in place.

In reading the passage about wanting only saints and teetotallers, it comes to mind that perhaps Bishop Grimes' insistence on Michael returning to Christchurch, is at some level a backhand compliment to Michael. After all, if he were not much good as a priest, or was inclined to drunkenness, would he have bothered? Or would his insistence on not allowing a 'test case' as he mentioned in his letter to Cardinal Moran, would this mindset have impelled him to secure Michael's return regardless of other factors?

Six of the ten priests in Wellington Diocese who had signed the petition did subsequently leave New Zealand: Joseph Ahern, Patrick Ahern, John Moore, James Prendergast, Andrew Cassidy and Richard O'Donnell. Archbishop Redwood it seems had no desire to retain disgruntled priests in his diocese. This would resonate with his offer to Father James O'Donnell to leave the diocese when he brought him back to Christchurch. Or perhaps he took note of the petition to Pope Leo XIII when the petitioners requested:

"If unfortunately our humble proposition cannot be executed, we humbly beg your holiness to inform His Excellency Monsignor the Archbishop of Wellington and His Excellency Monsignor Grimes bishop of Christchurch that they should follow all obligations as we have attached in their respective sees of Wellington and Christchurch and that they agree to grant us testimonial letters so that we can have the right to be able to seek elsewhere the justice they have continuously refused us here."

By way of contrast, of the eight signatories in Christchurch Diocese, only Michael left New Zealand. One other, Thomas Walsh transferred to Wellington, which was also a Marist Diocese, so probably considered an 'internal transfer'. Whether any of the others sought permission to leave isn't recorded, but given the difficulty Michael experienced, any who did were likely to have been refused in no uncertain terms. Bishop Grimes certainly did not take on board the request of the petitioners for testimonial letters to enable a move elsewhere.

Bishop Grimes, in his letter to Cardinal Moran in December 1890, says of Michael's complaints about his treatment by the Marists:

"As your eminence is well aware I am in no way responsible for this."

In saying he was not responsible there is a tacit acknowledgement that he was aware that there were problems. However, he made no effort to say how he was responding to the situation, if at all.

The Marist perspective

The Marists had their own take on the conflict, which as might be imagined, saw things very differently.

According to the Fraser[2] thesis, in 1886, thirty-six Marist priests who had gathered in Wellington for their annual retreat addressed a petition to Cardinal Simeoni, the Prefect of Propaganda, in which they expressed alarm at the prospect of the appointment of the secular Bishop Moran of Dunedin as archbishop of New Zealand and the consecration of a secular priest to the new see of Christchurch. Dunedin was not central and had fewer priests, people and church buildings than Wellington, they said. Moreover, they continued, Bishop Moran was neither a wise nor appropriate choice for the position of archbishop as he lacked the eloquence, tact and moderation needed.

The petition went on to say that with a secular bishop in Christchurch, conflicts would inevitably arise with the Society of Mary to whom Rome had granted several parishes in perpetuity.

Christchurch archives provided copies of letters written by the Marist priest, Father Le Menant de Chesnais. These provide further evidence of Marist disquiet and dissatisfaction with Dr. Moran.

3rd Nov 1887 to Marist Father Sauzeau:

"The articles of The New Zealand Tablet have done a great deal of harm and I am sure Dr. Moran would shed tears of sorrow if he fully comprehended the evil he has done and the prejudices against the Marists are so strong that we shall require God's special protection in order to destroy them."

Dr. Moran was instrumental in setting up *The Tablet*, which was very pro Irish seculars. It certainly was not always an impartial reporter.

17 Dec 1887, also to Fathe Sauzeau:

"For your presence here is sadly wanted and by letter it would be difficult to explain the painful situation we are now placed in. The presence of Fr O'Donnell here will revive and strengthen I believe, the prejudices against Dr Grimes and the society which were considerably diminished and nearly forgotten by the best people of our congregation. For his justification Fr O'Donnell thinks he is bound to state why he has been removed from his parish and been appointed as a curate in Christchurch. The people will look upon him as a victim and it will intensify their dislike for his Grace and the society. Such a nomination at the very time we were preparing a good reception for Dr Grimes and had fairly succeeded to enlist public opinion in our favour is, I repeat, most calamitous. However, since God has permitted it, we must submit to his holy will. Sit nomen Domini benedictum."

22 Dec 1887 to Archbishop Redwood:

"It is a great pity Dr Grimes has been detained so long in Europe; his presence here is absolutely necessary to settle several questions of vital importance. Your grace might have perceived how Father O'Donnell is looked upon as a victim of his patriotism and a kind of martyr. His presence here has greatly revived the discontent which existed against Dr. Grimes and the Marists and had in great measure been subdued. Fr O'Donnell makes no mystery to anyone that your grace demoted him because he signed the address to Dr Moran, that you told him his career would be ruined (blasted) forever in the diocese of Wellington and Christchurch, that you offered him his papers which he would not accept because he was not prepared to go but that he would not trouble you very long. The fact of Fr O'Donnell having been here before makes his case look worse than it would otherwise in Ireland, Australia and America. Your Grace, the Marists are being reported as enemies of Ireland and of the Irish priests. It may be for our greater spiritual good, but meanwhile it is a sore trial. When Fr O'Donnell is accepted by another bishop he will leave from the diocese triumphantly and with the sympathies of the Irish population. To remove him at present would be injudicious except a parish were given to him, and this again would be to acknowledge you had acted wrongly in taking his parish from him. Fr O'Donnell has a poor idea of the Marist brothers, he said the other day at table they were not fit to teach. If he thus speaks before the people, the consequences will be most fatal. I leave to your grace to say what should be done and I hope God will guide you how to act for the glory of God, of the society and the interest of Dr Grimes."

Father Le Menant de Chasnais writes that Father O'Donnell said he would not trouble Archbishop Redwood very long. Was he planning to leave after a time? And did he apply to Bishop Grimes for an *exeat* but found that door firmly closed? Perhaps he did, but there is no record. What is clear from Christchurch archives is that he did not subsequently leave the diocese.

It is also clear from Archbishop Redwood's letter of 13th December 1889, when he writes:

I would ask you to carefully preserve, <u>particularly</u>, his last letter where he gives the real motive of all his conduct, the so-called grievience against the Marist Fathers. This document may be of great use on some future occasion.

that he doesn't think much of Michaels comments on the treatment of Seculars by Marists. No hint of recognition of the problem there.

No early resolution

The conflict rumbled on. There were more appeals to Rome. In 1907 Propaganda Fide wrote to Bishop Grimes:

"Several times in these recent years the secular priests of the Christchurch diocese have complained about the conditions of their priestly lives and their financial support, and their complaints can be reduced to three. Diocesan priests are just helpers to religious, having no voice in the bishop's council; only the poorer parishes are allocated to them; it seems that there is discrimination against diocesan priests whose peace of mind is thus seriously disturbed."

So the message did get through to Rome. However, the Marists it seems still failed to deal with the problems as the difficulties continued for many more years after 1907. Further discussion of Secular / Marist discord is beyond the scope of this book.

Appendix II – Petition to Pope Leo XIII

(Translated from the French original)

To be presented under the patronage and the favour of

The most Eminent and Illustrious Cardinal Simeoni

Prefect of the holy congregation for Propaganda

To our most holy Father in God, Pope Leo XIII

Bishop of Rome and Vicar of Jesus Christ

Successor of St. Peter, Prince of the Apostles, Supreme Pontiff of the Universal Church

The Humble Petition of the undersigned secular priests of the former diocese of Wellington, New Zealand now of the Archepiscopal See of Wellington and of the diocese of Christchurch most submissively and respectfully shewith:

That having obtained satisfactory testimonial and demissorial letters from the Ordinaries of our various native Sees (mostly in Ireland) we became affiliated to the former diocese of Wellington with the tacit understanding that we should receive the same general treatment as other priests who ministered to the spiritual wants of the faithful in the same diocese.

That it was with this implicit understanding we all, or the greater numbers of us bound ourselves to the missionary oath.

That when we agreed to leave home and native country for the purpose of devoting our lives to the service of God and his Holy Church in this distant land, we had not even the most remote suspicion that any unjust or degrading discrimination would be made against secular priests in order to promote the greater temporal profit and advantage of the religious priests of the Society of Mary who likewise labour here.

That when coming hither we confidingly believed that we were destined to share with our brother priests of the Society of Mary not only in the hardships dangers and privations of missionary life, but also in a fair and just proportion of the emoluments of the missions whereby we might be enabled to make due provision for the necessities inseparable from infirmity and old age.

That after having travelled to the antipodes and having spent some time in the discharge of our missionary duties we learned with surprise and dismay that a very unjust and degrading discrimination had been secretly made against us, whereby we were to be perpetually excluded from no less than fourteen of the most desirable missionary districts in said diocese, these fourteen comprising nearly all the districts which yield more than a bare subsistence for the pastor.

That the pain and astonishment caused by this news were much further intensified when we were informed by some of the Marist priests that, relying on the representations and yielding to the requests made on behalf of the Society by a representative thereof in Rome, the Sacred Congregation of the Propaganda had actually confirmed the said Society in the exclusive and perpetual positions of these 14 missionary districts - to the great loss and degradation of the secular priests.

That supposing the information supplied to us on this subject to be true and exact: then we believe that the Sacred Congregation of The Propaganda must have been insufficiently informed or misinformed with regard to our existence and rights in the diocese; because otherwise it would appear inconceivable that so great an injustice and degradation would have been inflicted upon us without giving us any previous notification of a proceeding which involved issues of such great importance to us, and without even affording us an opportunity of speaking in defence of our threatened rights.

That this is all the more noteworthy as the secular priests constituted one-half of the working missionary staff of the diocese at the time the said concessions to the Marist Society are alleged to have been made.

That the missionary districts alluded to are as follows viz: Wellington, Christchurch, Napier, Wanganui, Meanee, Hastings, Timaru, Waimate, Temuka, Nelson Blenheim, Reefton, Greymouth and Hokitika

That having received no official information regarding these alleged perpetual concessions, we have, in the foregoing enumeration followed the list unofficially supplied to us by members of the Society of Mary.

That we have strong reasons for believing that, in representations made to the Sacred Congregation of The Propaganda, when the aforesaid concessions were sought for the Marist Society, six of the aforementioned missionary districts were fraudulently grouped together so as to make them appear in Rome as constituting only two whereas in reality they number six thoroughly distinct districts, each of which has had for years its own special resident pastor, its own quasi-parochial church, its boundaries fully defined, its special and separate quasi-parochial rights and obligations as well as its accounts and finances quite distinct and separate

That the groupings here referred to are: 1st, Napier, Meanee and Hastings as one group and alleged to have been wrongly represented as constituting only one of the missionary districts situated in the North Island: and 2nd, Timaru, Waimate and Temuka as another group similarly misrepresented as constituting only one of the missionary districts in the South Island

That because we lack official information upon this as well as upon other important points, we do not presume to affirm that this grouping and misrepresentation has been actually done; but we emphatically declare that if it has been done, it is grossly deceptive; and that the whole number of missionary districts thus perpetually placed beyond the reach of secular priests is in reality fourteen - not ten only, as would be made apparent by the aforesaid stratagem of grouping and misrepresentation

That since the Archbishop of Wellington and the Bishop of Christchurch are both Marists, we believe the two Cathedral congregations in Wellington and Christchurch respectively, may be fairly looked upon for the present as being likewise practically conceded to the Marist Society, since the said Society is secured in the possession of them at least during the lives of these Prelates. Thus, the number of important concessions made to the Marist Society (to our disadvantage) amounts to 16.

That during the Plenary Council of Sydney in November 1885 we sent in a complaint which embodied the grievances herein stated, and which was duly delivered to the Most Rev Dr Redwood who was then acting as a member of the Central Committee of the Plenary Council. That having received no satisfactory answer to that complaint, we renewed and restated the same in a joint address which we personally presented to His Lordship, when assembled for the annual retreat at Christchurch in the month of February 1886

225

That His Lordship then promised to consider the various matters complained of and to send us a full reply in the shape of a circular letter, a copy of which he would mail to each of us.

That none of us has yet received the promised circular letter.

That while we make no complaint about the fact of our having been placed in the most laborious and (in a worldly sense) the least remunerative missions in the diocese, while we are still strong in health, and able to endure much hardship and privation, we cannot but regard as a very serious evil the prospect of being continuously confined as we advance in years to these very laborious missions which yield only a bare sustenance; while some more-favoured Marists whose term of service in the diocese is shorter than our own, and others of the same Society who have not yet arrived here, are either already promoted, or destined to be promoted above our heads, to places of comparative ease and large emoluments - places to which we, degraded seculars, dare not aspire under the present regulations.

That the missionary districts of which the secular priests have charge are in reality very much poorer than might be supposed at first sight, especially if in making an estimate of them a person were to judge merely from the statistics of population and revenue. That in order to form a true and correct estimate of any given missionary district, it is necessary to consider the area of territory which it embraces, quite as carefully as its population and revenue. This necessity of attending to area is due to the seemingly paradoxical fact that, generally speaking, the larger the area the smaller the revenue and of course the more laborious the work of the mission.

That in most cases the missionary districts confided to secular priests are aggregations of very small missions scattered over very large territories, and singly so insignificant that it takes, as a rule, from two to five or six or even a greater number of them to constitute what the Bishop judges to be sufficient for a priest's maintenance. That these little missions are usually so widely separated from one another that a priest cannot generally speaking attend to more than one or at most two of them on any Sunday.

That one obvious consequence of this is that the priest being able to bring together for Holy Mass or Vespers only one half, one fourth, one sixth or even a smaller proportion of the people confided to his care, he accordingly receives only one half, one quarter or one sixth (as the case may be) of the Sunday collections which he would otherwise receive from the whole people confided to him, had they been living in such proximity to one another that they could all assemble at the same church and attend at Holy Mass every Sunday and festival of obligation.

That besides this the heavy expenses of railway fares, cost and maintenance of horses, trappings and vehicles, added to hotel bills as well as grooms fees and stable charges - all unavoidably entailed by the duty of almost constantly travelling from one to another of these numerous, small and widely separated missions usually absorb all or the greater part of the offerings a priest receives on his missionary tours.

That thus it is plain that the <u>compactness</u> of a congregation limited within a <u>small area</u> greatly enhances the value of the support derivable therefrom over and above what might be judged from the figures indicating population and revenue; while on the other hand the <u>dispersion</u> of another mission which is spread over a very large area greatly minimises that statistical value of its revenue - 1st by lessening the possibility of Sunday receipts; and 2nd by the necessity of consuming, on travelling expenses, the limited offerings received.

That in view of these facts it is important to observe that the fourteen (or sixteen) congregations conceded to the Marist Society (and from the pastoral charge of which, accordingly, the secular priests are to be forever excluded) are for the most part the larger seaport cities and towns - a circumstance which secures them the twofold benefit of large <u>compact congregations in a small area</u> with little or <u>no necessity of travelling</u> frequently or far from home.

That while the Marist Priests have laudably erected a splendid and costly home, with ample means of sustenance attached, to serve as a retreat wherein the aged and infirm priests of their Society may spend the evening of their lives in peaceful rest and prayer, it is lamentable fact that there is no provision whatever made for secular priests who become invalided on the mission.

That to provide against the suffering and destitution onto which infirmity or accident might precipitate some of us at any time we made an attempt to establish a fund for the maintenance of infirm secular priests in the month of June 1883.

That owing to the fact of all the secular priests being very poor, and their regular income being barely sufficient to meet their actual wants, and therefore utterly inadequate to the establishment and efficient maintenance of an infirm priests fund, we decided to request our Bishop's permission for an annual collection to be made for the benefit of the proposed 'Infirm Priests' Fund' in such of the missionary districts as were receiving the services of secular priests.

That his Lordship Dr Redwood SM at first kindly favoured our project and said he had much pleasure in granting the permission sought for the purpose of aiding the establishment and maintenance of the proposed infirm priests fund.

That the deputation who waited on his Lordship on behalf of the whole body of secular priests returned rejoicing and speedily announced his favourable reply which filled the hearts of their brother priests with joy and gratitude – but

That their joy was short-lived; because in a few days afterwards His Lordship revoked the permission so lately given stating as his reason for the withdrawal thereof that some of the Marist Fathers objected to the proposed collection; and that since the collection could not be allowed everywhere according to the rule proposed, he would not permit it to be made in any congregation whatever in his diocese

That our endeavour on behalf of infirm secular priests having thus failed, no provision of any kind for their safety or comfort has ever since been made.

That owing to the consequent absence of any means of relief for such of us as have the misfortune of suffering loss of health, two of our number who became incapacitated for duty within the past 18 months have been obliged to depart hence and are now dragging out a wretched existence in squalid poverty elsewhere

That while we sadly deplore the hard fate of our beloved brother priests, who have dropped down in our ranks without any fault of their own, we strongly deprecate the system of diocesan administration which negligently and (as we believe) culpably permits such hardship and thus practically consigns priests of good character and many merits to untold misery and destitution

That under the existing regulations we are all exposed to the same evil fate which has already befallen our more unfortunate brothers, as an accident resulting from any of the numerous dangerous which we constantly encounter by "flood and field", may at any time incapacitate us for duty; or we may, in the natural course of things, lose our health and thus become a prey to unsightly indigence

That in consequence of having repeatedly protested against the injustices herein complained of, we have, to our sorrow, incurred the grave displeasure, and in some instances the bitter resentment, not to say the odious hostility of the Marist Fathers, who appear to entertain a very reasonable fear that we may yet win back those rights of which they despoiled us by dark and surreptitious means

That since (as is well known to the Marist priests) it is our firm unalterable determination to continue protesting against these injustices so long as any of us lives, or until just and adequate redress is obtained; the antagonism which unfortunately now exists in the diocese between the Marist priests on the one side and the secular priests on the other, is so far from diminishing that it is likely to grow apace and may if no timely and adequate remedy be applied, result in grave scandal - which may God mercifully avert

That the antagonism alluded to is particularly distressing to young secular priests who are serving as curates under Marist pastors, and are of course often obliged to live in the same house, eat at the same table and to associate intimately in countless ways with their Marist superiors, who in many cases regard them with much aversion (to speak mildly) and who have power to make the said secular curates feel their (the Marists) displeasure in numberless ways.

That we believe the practice of placing secular priests in the position of curates under Marist pastors is irregular and it is strictly forbidden by the Superior General of the Marist Society.

That owing to the antagonism already alluded to, all or the greater number of those mission stations where there are Marist pastors and secular curates are in the condition of 'a house divided against itself'.

That the Marist Society's penchant for placing all their available priests in the pastoral charges of these numerous important missions from which secular curates must be kept excluded (besides others about which there is no controversy) has necessitated the placing of secular curates in Marist Mission stations notwithstanding the Superior General's prohibition.

That probably the worst of the many evils arising from the antagonism between Marists and seculars lies in the fact that the secular priests considered themselves bereft of the benefits of an unprejudiced ecclesiastical court in the diocese or even in the newly formed province of New Zealand, since both the Archbishop of Wellington (now Metropolitan) and the Bishop of Christchurch are Marists and as such presumably prejudiced against the secular priests on account of this wretched controversy - the Prelates themselves being in the position of interested and joint litigants against the said secular of priests.

That under these circumstances and during the present unhappy state of strong feeling it appears a very incongruous proceeding to put a secular priest on his trial before a Marist priest delegated to act as judge in the Bishops Palace and to exercise the Bishop's authority in passing judgement upon his secular antagonist, yet such proceedings have taken place here in several instances of recent occurrence.

That the secular priests have patiently borne the wrongs herein complained of for several years; and that they have hitherto refrained from making an appeal to the Holy See, for the following reasons, to with

Firstly: we fondly nourished the delusive hope that we might obtain redress from our own Bishop; and we looked upon an appeal to Rome as an extreme proceeding which should not be resorted to until all other hopes and means of redress have proved ineffectual.

Secondly: we sincerely desired to live in peace and friendship with our brother priests of the Marist Society, and we firmly believed that our making an appeal to the Holy See would provoke much more ill feeling on their part and would not only cause much greater estrangement between ourselves and the Marist Fathers, but that it would put a further heavy strain upon the ties which bound (and still bind) us in love, honour and obedience to our Bishop.

Thirdly: we greatly dreaded (and still dread) the consequences of incurring our Bishop's (now Archbishop's) extreme displeasure, which as we firmly believed (and as we still believe) would be provoked by appealing to the Holy See. The same dread even still deters several of us from signing this Petition and those who sign it will do so with sorrow and trepidation.

That now at length, having abandoned all other hope and being in a state of deplorable misgiving in regard to our future prospects here, we turn our eyes and our hearts imploringly towards Apostolic Rome and place all the hope that remains to us in the highest and last Tribunal on Earth. Woe betide us if we are doomed to failure and disappointment. Our condition will be if possible much worse than before.

With the greatest submissiveness and in a most supplicant manner we come to the feet of Your Holiness to suggest a remedy for our distress and misfortune, the only remedy that seems to us at once simple, practical and effective, is the following:

That all the Marist priests are sent to one diocese, Wellington or Christchurch as _they_ prefer and that they have the complete, total, exclusive and perpetual possession of all the missions and properties of the diocese they choose, if that pleases the Holy See and that all the secular priests are placed in the other diocese which we ask Your Holiness to secularise and that they are treated on their merit like all other missionaries of good reputation and ability.

That in making respectfully this suggestion, we strive to imitate the example of our father Abraham, by following as best we can the rules of condescendence and self denial in a spirit of charity which appear to us directed at ending the quarrels that arose between his herdsmen and those of his nephew Lot.

That we secular priests now wish to treat our brother Marist priests in the same spirit of conciliation, of fraternal charity, and the love of peace. O Blessed! Harmonious! Heavenly Peace!!! We desire to address them in the words of the same Patriarch and to say to them from the bottom of our heart:

"I pray thee let there be no strife between me and thee, and between my herdsmen and your herdsmen, for we are brothers. Behold the whole land before you, separate yourself from me I pray you. If you will go to the left hand, then I will go to the right. If you choose the right, I will go left." Gen XIII, 8 and 9

If unfortunately our humble proposition cannot be executed, we humbly beg your holiness to inform His Excellency Monsignor the Archbishop of Wellington and His Excellency Monsignor Grimes bishop of Christchurch that they should follow all obligations as we have attached in their respective sees of Wellington and Christchurch and that they agree to grant us testimonial letters so that we can have the right to be able to seek elsewhere the justice they have continuously refused us here.

Prostrate in spirit before Your Holiness, we bow with the greatest reverence at Your Apostolic Feet and with the most patient submission we hope for and await the decision of Supreme authority.

May the decision on our petition be favourable but if not we pray ardently that it may please Your Holiness to afford us an apostolic blessing.

We sign as the most humble and obedient servants, children in need and pleading petitioners to Your Holiness.

Name –	Residence –	Diocese
J O'Donnell –	Christchurch –	Christchurch
M Macmanus –	Ross –	Christchurch
J L Ahern –	Waipawa –	Wellington
P W Ahern –	Kaikoura –	Wellington
Joseph Lane –	Lower Hutt –	Wellington
A C Cassidy –	New Plymouth –	Wellington
H G Bowers –	Geraldine –	Christchurch
M C Kickham –	Lyttelton –	Christchurch
Michael D Browne -	Timaru –	Christchurch
John Moore –	Te-Aro (Wellington) -	Wellington
Patrick Power –	St Mary's Cathedral –	Wellington
John McKenna -	Masterton -	Wellington
James McKenna –	Howera -	Wellington
R O'Donnell –	Nelson –	Wellington
J P Prendergast –	Napier –	Wellington
Thomas Walsh –	Kumara –	Christchurch
D O'Hallahan –	Ahaura –	Christchurch
P Treacy –	Kumara –	Christchurch

Dated Festival of St Thomas Aquinas, 1888

Notes

Chapter 1 – Firstborn Son
Chapter 2 - Last Rites
1. Dominican priests from Lacordaire College, Fathers Murphy and Owens were recorded as having attended the wedding of Louisa and John Feeney. See also Chapter 14
2. Fr. Francis was mentioned in Tom's letter to Kattie. See also Chapter 15
3. Dr. Pennington is named on the death certificate as the attending doctor.
Chapter 3 - Michael's story
1. Report on preaching NZ Tablet 2nd July 1886
Chapter 4 - Mullinahone
1. The lines are from "The Two Travellers" by C J Boland
2. Names of godparents recorded in Church baptismal records
Chapter 5 - Being a Kickham –
1. "Charles Kickham a biography" by RV Comerford records the various firearm accidents as well as other aspects of the life of Charles J Kickham.
2. Charles Kickham's niece, Annie, in a letter dated 30th December 1937 to Kattie Murphy *neé* Kickham, sister of Michael, recalled that she and Michael were playmates in their childhood, before Kattie was born.
Chapter 6 – A Vocation
1. Two books on Mount Mellary provided background information: "The History of Mount Mellary" by Stephen J. Molony O. Cist.; and "History of the Foundation of Mount Melleray" by Dom Vincent de Paul Ryan
2. The story of C. is a fiction.
3. Background information on All Hallows, including details of the annual entrance exam, from "The Missionary College of All Hallows 1842-1891" by Kevin Condon c.m.
4. A half note – a pound note cut in two, one half sent initially, the other half later: a security measure – stealing a half note was useless, you needed both halves
5. Cars referred to were horse drawn. There were no motor cars in Ireland at the time
6. Vincent Comerford, in his biography of C J Kickham, records that Archbishop Croke nominated a confessor for CJK.
7. Comerford refers to a letter of condolences from the Archbishop to Alexander Kickham and the details surrounding the burial – locked gate, PP absence and antipathy to Fenians, his illness etc.
8. Comerford mentions that a clerical student recited the *De Profundis*. The student is not named, but family lore has it that it was Michael.
9. There is no evidence that Michael saw the letter from Melleray.
10. Information on Le Grand Seminaire and the Suplician Way obtained from web

searches.

11. POO stands for Post Office Order

12. Michael's records, received from All Hallows archives, show that he was conferred with sub-deaconate and deaconate *in absentia* and that he received a Holy See dispensation for early ordination.

13. Ordination details from book on All Hallows referenced above.

14. Details re Michael's first mass in Mullinahone presumed.

Chapter 7 - To the Antipodes

1. Itinerary of the Garonne from archives.

2. Ceremonies of this nature were common when crossing the equator.

3. That Michael said Mass in the Cathedral in Melbourne is recorded in The Advocate, 25 October 1884.

4. Account of first days assumed from available historical information.

Chapter 8 - New Zealand

1. Christmas prizegiving Hawkes Bay Herald 20 Dec '84.

2. Fr. Reignier jubilee Hawkes Bay Herald 2 Jan '85.

3. Temp assignment to Wairoa while Fr. Ahern was away - Manawatu Standard 8 Jan '85.

4. Maori information from the web.

5. Feast of St. Michael celebration NZ Tablet 16 Oct. '85.

6. Birthday celebration NZ Tablet 13 Nov 85 and Hawkes Bay Herald 3 Nov 85.

7.Soggarth aroon: from the Irish *Sagart a rún* – dear priest

8. Report on Michaels departure: Napier Evening News 5th March 1887.

9. Mr. Hornsby had previously chaired of a meeting on Home Rule: Hawkes Bay Herald 6th July 1886.

10. Date of Bishop Grimes appointment from Christchurch archives.

11. Fr. O'Donnell's dismissal from Ahaura is mentioned in a letter from Fr. Le Menant de Chesnais to Fr Sauzeau, both Marists, 17 Dec '87, in which he writes Fr. O'Donnell said Bishop Redwood told him his career would be 'blasted' and offered him permission to leave NZ - from Christchurch archives; see also Appendix I – Secular Priests and Marists;

12. Fr. O'Donnell presentation at Ahuara NZ Tablet 16 Mar '88; presentation of trap, ibid. 7 Dec '88.

13. NZ Tablet 10 Feb '88

14. It seems Fr. O'Donnell was the prime mover of the petition. The actual petition was written in French, reason unknown. A draft of the petition received from Christchurch archives had been annotated by Bishop Grimes, listing those who had signed and noting the names of a few who were against it, and others who had not been approached because they might not maintain confidentiality. I have no idea how the Bishop got a copy of the draft or the names of those who did and

didn't sign. The draft was incomplete but only a small portion was missing. There was no difference between the draft and the final version, apart from translation to French.

15. Celebrations NZ Tablet 20 Mar, 30 Mar 88.

16. Rebuke from altar NZ Tablet 6 Apr '88, Follow up re B. Grimes rebuke to MCK on St. Patrick's Day celebrations ibid.

17. NZ Tablet 13 Jan '88

18. Duke of Norfolk's Crowd: Liberal Intellectuals and Public Culture in Modern Britain 1815 to 1914 by William C. Lubenow.

19. NZ Tablet 8 June 1888

20. Report on official visit: Lyttelton Times, 19 June 1888

21. Thrown from a horse: Akaroa Mail 15 June 1888.

22. Report on fundraiser: NZ Tablet 21 September 1888

23. letter from Christchurch archives

24. NZ Tablet 4 Feb 1889

25. The Star 25 Feb 1889

26. Akaroa Mail and Banks Peninsula Advertiser 26 Feb 1889

27. NZ Tablet 8 March 1889

28. Report on St. Patrick's Day celebration: The Star, 19 March 1889

29. Catholics of Lyttelton farewell: NZ Tablet 23 March 1889

30. Two words no longer in common use: preceptor – teacher for upholding a particular tradition; precentor – choir leader

31. NZ Tablet 12 Apr. 1889

Chapter 9 - Jesuit Novice

1. Jesuits in Kew provided a copy of the diary for the period Michael was there. Items shown are those referring to Michael.

Chapter 10 - *Exeat*

1. NZ Tablet 14 Sep 1888

2. Michael's letters received from Christchurch archives

3. £200 in 1889 is equivalent to over €31,000 in 2021, taking account of inflation and currency changes (Pound to Punt to Euro) over the years since.

4. Documents from Christchurch archives state that in 1874 Bishop Grimes had been sent to teach at Jefferson College, Louisiana. While helping in the Yellow Fever outbreak there in 1878, he caught the fever, which affected his health thereafter.

Yellow fever had weakened his (Bishop Grimes) health, and within two years of his arrival (he had arrived in February 1888) he was critically ill. It was typical of his resilience that he turned the convalescent voyage to Europe into an official visit to Rome, and made his return journey a fact-finding tour of North America.

His welcome back to Christchurch in September 1891 was a demonstration of affection in contrast to the formal courtesy of his first reception. [from Te Ara, Dictionary of New Zealand biography]

5. Copy of the Bishop's letter to the Cardinal received from Sydney archive and the Cardinal's reply from Christchurch archive. There is no evidence that the Cardinal showed the letters to Michael, but it allows their introduction.

6. Copy of Archbishop Redwood's reply to Bishop Grimes on the granting of a conditional *exeat*. It is inconceivable that Michael would ever have known of that letter. The statement that he learned of it later is included purely to allow its introduction in Michael's narrative.

Chapter 11 – Australia

1. Meeting Fr Prendergast: Daily Telegraph 25 Feb 1890.

2. Full details of the murder, trial and execution were reported in Mount Alexander Mail 18 Nov 1891 and many other newspapers. Michael's views on capital punishment are not recorded.

3. The visit of Br. Joseph was recorded NZ Tablet 1 April 1892.

4. First half of letter hasn't survived. Date can be estimated by reference to when Tom left All Hallows and date of Charles Kickham's anniversary in August

5. Not known if Michael saw Tom's letter re change from All Hallows, but probably did.

6. Information on the asylum and the orphanage from the web.

7. Freemans Journal 21 Mar '96

8. Camden News 10 Oct 1895;

9. Oaks sports: Camden News 14 Nov 1895, 30 July '96 and 12 Oct '96

10. Departing Camden: Camden News 24 November 1898.

11. Freeman's Journal 27th Aug 1898

12. Hotel gathering and platform good-bye: Daily Telegraph 6th May '99. Michael's speech at departure event not reported, author's assumption based on his many other speeches.

13. There are no records of any discussions between Michael and Fr. Comerford. See also chapter Enigma.

Chapter 12 - Ireland

1. Copy of gun licence – see photo

2. Kattie and Ramie's marriage certificate states they were married in Waterford Cathedral, there is actually no information as to how this was arranged. Neither of them had Waterford city connections.

3. Vincentian archives provided details of Tom's assignments

4. No evidence exists of Michael being hospitalised or meeting Ramsey Nixon or Dr. Gray in 1900. Author's assumption. Newspaper reports place Dr. Gray at St. Helens Hospital. Passenger lists identify timing of Ramsey Nixon's departure for Punta Arenas. Their meeting in 1900 (if it happened) provides a basis for their meeting in Punta Arenas in 1905, which is on record.

5. Brentford Diocese archives confirmed that Fr. McKenna was in Rome for the month Michael was in Southend on Sea, and that he had been in the Irish College in Paris while Michael was in Angers. Both were ordained in 1884.

6. Letter from Anne Kirby (see chapter 17 - Enigma), while not conclusive, strongly suggests he had been in hospital. That he was cared for in Melleray is author's assumption. Melleray did confirm that longer stays were occasionally allowed, however there were no specific records.

7. It is not recorded whether Michael told anyone he was leaving the priesthood.

8. Information on C. J. Boland from web. "The Two Travellers" was published in 1906. Whether Michael learned of it in Buenos Aires is not known. However it is a favourite of the author, it relates to the narrative, so the assumption has been made that he did come across it.

Chapter 13 - Buenos Ayres

1. Not much is known of Michael's life in BA apart from friendship with Louisa Feeney neé Moughty and that he opened a school. Descendents of the Feeneys and Moughtys in Ireland provided background information. Searches on Irish genealogy and the 1901 census provided additional information. The marriage cert of Anne Moughty and James Feeney identifies Anne's home as being Ballinacargy. Information from Vincentian archives confirms Fr. O'Farrell was also from Ballinacargy.

"Irish Argentine Identity in an Age of Political Challenge and Change" by Patrick Speight provided background information on the kind of society Irish emigrants found in Argentina in the early 1900s.

2. Michael's sign-in to the British Club in Punta Arenas was discovered on a web search. Both he and a Dr. F A. Gray from Armagh were signed in by the same person on 7 January 1905. They were almost certainly travelling together, there is no other obvious explanation. The signature of the member who signed them in was illegible, but the British Club confirmed the member was Ramsey. B. Nixon, and that one of them would have had to have known Ramsey to be admitted. Details of Ramsey's position in Punta Arenas, his new appointment in Valparaiso and his imminent departure for Valparaiso and date of same were reported in the local newspaper 'El Comercio'. Valparaiso English Language newspaper 'Star of Chile' carried a light-hearted report on the Christmas celebrations aboard the *Oropesa* voyage which included a reference to the ships doctor, Dr. F A Gray, an Irishman. Check on Irish Civil Records records the birth in Armagh of one Francis Auboden Gray in 1872, father a doctor. The *Oropesa* arrived in Punta Arenas on the morning of 7 January and departed that evening or the following day for Valparaiso with Ramsey Nixon on Board. How Michael Kickham came to be there is a mystery, however the narrative of him meeting them in 1900 and an invitation from Dr. Gray to join him on the voyage at Montevideo is considered a plauaible explanation.

3. At Punta Norte on the Peninsula de Valdes Southern Right Whales and Orcas are regularly sighted, and Elephant Seals breed there.

4. The area around Puerto Madryn, Trelew, Rawson and Gaiman became a place of immigration for many Welsh people after 1865. Welsh is still spoken and there is a proudly Welsh community in the area, also further up the Chubut river valley towards the Andes, around the town of Trevelin.

5. Information on Punta Arenas in the 1890s from *Madhouse at the end of the earth* by Julian Sancton, a book on a Belgian Antarctic Expedition.

6. Tom's letter to Katty of June 1910, states that it was Louisa and her husband who first made it known that Michael was in Buenos Ayres. Background information from the Moughty and Feeney families leads to approximate date of this. Date of passage of John and Luisa to Buenos Ayres, 6 Sep 1907 from Southampton, obtained from Donna Moughty in the US. Louisa therefore arrived in BA sometime in October 1907, just over two years before Michael died. A letter to Ireland would have taken some six weeks, a reply to BA a further six weeks, plus time for Fr. O'Farrell to contact Tom and to receive a reply from him together with letter for Michael. Adding up all the timelines led me to suggest sometime in February 1908. How the letter from Tom was transmitted to Michael, or the circumstances of same, or how Michael reacted to the news, are not known.

7. Wedding of John and Luisa, 29th April 1908, reported in Buenos Ayres newspaper Southern Cross. It records that Frs. Owens and Murphy were present, that John and Luisa received a present of a house from John's brothers and that the wedding celebrations after the Church were in Quinta Las Rosas, home of James and Anne Feeney. It also gives the name of the person who had owned the property Louisa and John received as a wedding gift from John's brothers. He was a doctor and the address was listed in a directory. This enabled me to establish the distance from Michael's apartment. Michael's presence at the wedding is not recorded but is assumed based on their friendship. Departure of the newly-weds for Ireland reported in the Southern Cross. Photos of houses from Feeney family.

8. As in almost everything about Michael's life in Buenos Ayres, no record exists of how Michael felt about having left Ireland. Southern Cross obituary refers to his last illness, suggesting there was a previous one.

Chapter 14 – Death

1. Dr. Stuart Pennington was a visiting physician at the British Hospital and is named on the death cert.

2. Southern Cross 7th Dec. 1909

3. Southern Cross 11th Dec. 1909

Chapter 15 – Six Months Later

1. I was born and lived the early years of my life at 12 O'Connell St, and can remember it quite vividly. Timothy Murphy and Annie Curran are recorded as living there in the 1911 census.

2. Transcript of actual nuptial agreement, original in author's possession

3. Erysipelas is an infection of the skin which could be fatal at the time, but is now easily treated with antibiotics.

4. My father, Anthony Murphy spoke often of Kattie's devout religion, and that she had prayed to St Anthony for his safe birth.

Chapter 16 – Enigma

No notes.

Chapter 17 – The Two Travellers

Date of publication of *The Two Travellers* c.1906, so it seems unlikely Michael was aware of its existence, although it is possible it circulated among the Irish community in Buenos Aires. It is a favourite of the author, hence references to it, which are in any case apposite. C. J. Boland was born 1864 and died in 1918. He was a civil servant in Dublin, hence the assumption of spending a lot of time on the Cork Dublin train which at the time followed the old Clonmel Thurles branch line, now long closed. His parents were Master and Matron of the Clonmel Workhouse. They lived at Tobberaheena between Clonmel and Marlfield, hence presumably the lines:

Don't talk of your hunting in Yucatan, Or your fishing off St Helena;
I'd rather see young fellows hunting the 'wran' In the hedges of Tobberraheena:

His nephew was F.H Boland, Ireland's representative to the UN and President of the General Assembly meeting during the Cuban missile crisis when Khrushchev famously removed his shoe and banged the table; F H Boland was later Chancellor of Trinity College Dublin; C. J. Boland's grand-niece, F H Boland's daughter, is renowned poet Eavan Boland.

Appendix I - Secular priests & Marists

1. Bishop Grimes: His Context and Contribution to the Catholic Church in Canterbury. B. S. Allom, University of Canterbury 1968

2. Community, Continuity and Change: Irish Catholic Immigrants in nineteenth-century Christchurch. Lyndon A. Fraser, University of Canterbury 1993

www.ingramcontent.com/pod-product-compliance
Lightning Source LLC
Chambersburg PA
CBHW021049090426
42738CB00006B/262